Spoonful of Courage is a thought-provoking and timely read. Chuck Page makes an ardent case for a Creator, emphasizing that we are each born with a purpose—even when that purpose turns out to be significantly different than we envisioned. When life deals us painful blows, God's inexplicable grace can still have a transformative impact on our lives and the lives of others around us.

ALI MASTER
Author of Beyond the Golden Door

Spoonful of Courage is a challenging apologetic for a worldview at variance with our popular culture and the spirit of the times. Dr. Page effectively uses poignant stories from his personal and professional life to illustrate the importance of confronting one's confirmation biases and the worthy pursuit of absolute Truth. This book exposes the fallacy of "doing" before "being." It is extremely well thought out and engaging at the same time. Regardless of your worldview, you should read this.

MARK D. BRUCE, DO
Author of Jackie, A Boy, and A Dog: A Warm Cold War Story

These formulas helped me grasp what it's all about. If you're trying to figure life out, *Spoonful of Courage* helps you put the pieces together in a cohesive, understandable way. And the stories challenged me to think deeply about how I respond in certain situations. This is a great book to give to a friend who's struggling with their faith—either with intellectual questions or with adversity.

JOE PETTIGREW
Author, Speaker, and CEO of In the Zone Ministries

Spoonful of Courage is not what you would expect from the pen (or laptop) of a surgeon. Dr. Page sees the whole person—mind, body, and spirit. He brings compassion, hope, and healing to medicine. And he encourages us to hold tightly to our faith during challenging physical times. This book blesses the heart and soul.

DR. BERNADETTE ANDERSON
Author, speaker, and founder of Life in Harmony

Our world has gone mad. Everything is in flux. Most of our lives have been turned upside down. We need someone sane to come in and bring some order to this chaos. We need hope, reassurance, guidance, and wisdom. Thankfully, Dr. Chuck Page has met some of that massive need with this book. Dr. Chuck's life equation not only makes sense—it works.

GARY ROE
Best-selling author and grief specialist

Your legs allow you to get from point A to point B. But only your brain determines the level of happiness and effectiveness of that trip. This book explains how to maximize that trip.

ALEXANDER KORELIN
Author, consultant, and host of the KER report radio show

In my eyes, Dr. Chuck is a humble genius! In addition to inspiring us with his stories of hope, he uses his experiences as a surgeon to formulate practical equations to assist us as we navigate the dis-ease of our own lives. He invites any and all to embrace the practical tools that God can use to transform our mind, body, and spirit—regardless of our circumstances.

HEATHER CARTER
Author, speaker, podcaster, and cancer survivor

"A mind is a terrible thing to waste." If you believe this, then this book is for you. Dr. Page's book has helped me categorize my thinking. Now I know when I am falling into one of my cognitive traps and how to get out of it. As you include all of the terms and factors he describes in this book, you'll gain the "thinking" sanity you have always wanted. Don't waste your mind or time anymore.

BRUCE DAVIS
President and Host of the In Awe Podcast

Spoonful of Courage is an easy read. It provides simple insights and habits you can implement into your everyday life. This book, which will help you live a more fulfilling, productive, and satisfying life, is highly recommended.

KENT BURDEN
Author of Is this Chair Killing You?

Charles W. Page, MD

Equations for Finding Grace in Life's Challenges

Spoonful of Courage
Equations for Finding Grace in Life's Challenges

Copyright 2022, Charles W. Page, MD

All rights reserved. No portion of this book may be reproduced, stored in a retrieval system, or transmitted in any form, or by any means—electronic, mechanical, photocopy, recording, scanning, or other—except for brief quotations in reviews or articles, without the prior written consent of the author.

Some names and identifying details have been changed to protect the anonymity of the individuals referred to in this book.

Published in Nacogdoches, TX by Spoonful of Courage LLC. Spoonful of Courage is a trademark of Dr. Charles Page and Spoonful of Courage LLC. For inquiries contact us at spoonfulofcourage.com.

Further mail and inquiries:
Spoonful of Courage LLC
Attn: Dr. Charles Page
1320 University
Nacogdoches, TX 75961

ISBN: 978-0-9997609-5-6 (e-book)
ISBN: 978-0-9997609-6-3 (paperback)

Illustrations by Georgia Anne Page

To my loving wife, Joanna.

To our Fabulous Five:
Jacob, Jonathan, Georgia, Jane-Aubrey, and Charlie.

To our second family,
the Wednesday night college students
and Bible study gang.

Thanks for reviving my hope.
Keep going, and remember,
there's never a circumstance too great
for an all-wise, all-loving
God of grace.

For an overview of the principles in this book, click below and register. When you sign up, you'll receive

- four short videos which explain the ways we see our circumstances and the ways in which we respond,
- a framework to transform your challenges into blessings and
- updates from the Spoonful of Courage TV show.

Register here for FOUR free videos

Contents

PART ONE

Chapter One 13
   The Nail in the Neck—Got to Go through It 13
   We're Going on a Journey 17
   A Peek into Part Two 17
   The Embedded Nail in Our Thinking 18
   The Fame, Blame, and Shame Game 19
   My Point of View 19

Chapter Two 21
   Choices and Consequences 21
   The Victim Equation 22
   The Victim Mindset 23
   I am No Exception 24
   Brandy the Bander 24

Chapter Three 29
   Who Wears the Boots? 29
   The Sum of Our Experiences 31
   Overwhelming Emotions 32
   Sinking into the Victim Mindset 33
   Trapped in the Analysis Paralysis 36

Chapter Four 39
   Please, Chop 'Em Off 39
   The Second Level of Thinking 40
   A Hero in the Strife 42
   The Power of Self-awareness 42
   The Power of Ingenuity 43
   The Power of Initiative 43

  The Power of Resourcefulness 44
  The Power of Adaptability 44
  The Power of an Unconquerable Spirit 45

Chapter Five 49
  We Have Met the Enemy and… 49
  The "Don't Make Me a Hero" Heroes 55
  Who's the Enemy? 55
  The Human Dilemma. 56

Chapter Six 59
  The Second-level See-saw. 59
  A Shocking Story 61
  The Second Guesser's See-saw 63
  Second-level Ambiguity 63

Chapter Seven 67
  Living a Lie or Having an Open Mind. 67
  The Source of the Matter. 69
  Forced to Hide a Secret 70
  The Issue Isn't the Issue 71

Summary of Part One. 73

PART TWO

Chapter Eight. 79
  Clues to a Higher Power 79
  A Diagnosis Looking for a Patient 80
  Intelligent Design 83
  Irreducible Complexity and Devolution 85
  Consciousness and Moral Obligation 87

Chapter Nine. 89
  The Puzzle Pieces and the Puzzle Box 89
  The Third Sphere: History 91
  Reliable Eyewitness Accounts 93

Chapter Ten 99
    Galileo, a Blind Man, and a Personal Secret 99
    A Geocentric Universe 99
    A Shift in Perspective 100
    The Qualities of a New Element 101
    Absolutes vs. Arbitrary Absolutes 101
    A Personal God 102
    Performance and Acceptance 103
    The G Factor 104
    The Life Equation 106
    The Power of the G Factor 106
    My "Come to Jesus" Meeting 107

Chapter Eleven 111
    An African Artist and a Truck Driver 111
    Defining the Outcome 112
    Knowing Who Helps with the Whys 113
    The E's Give Everything Needed 114
    Unanticipated Outcomes 117

Chapter Twelve 121
    Wally, an Old Table, and a Doorkeeper 121
    Where's Wally? 121
    A Dose of Favor 122
    Grace Influences Our Circumstances 123
    Opportunities for Growth 124
    Opportunities to Relate to God 124
    Opportunities to Impact Others 124
    The Rest of Nick's Story 126

Chapter Thirteen 129
    Elliot and the Baggage Carrier. 129
    Determining Our Level 131
    Who's in Control? 131
    Where's the Focus? 132
    Who Gets the Credit? 134
    Who Carries the Burden? 134

Chapter Fourteen 139
   Significant or Special?. 139
   Assessing the Source of Our Esteem. 140
   How Does God See Us? 141
   Esteeming Others More Than Ourselves 142
   What am I feeling? 144
   What Do We Fear? 146
   Listening to Our Language 147

Chapter Fifteen 151
   Ayudame Carlos. Taking Small Steps of Faith 151
   An Invitation 155
   Lower-level Responses. 156
   A Common Circumstance 157
   The G Factor Brings Good News 158
   Two Possible Responses 159

Chapter Sixteen 163
   Farmers, Bankers, and More Machetes. 163
   Acceptance 165
   Acknowledgment 166
   Adjustment. 167
   Anticipation 168
   Four Helpful Resources 168
   Another Machete at Bongolo 170

Your Formula and Your Story 175
   What's Your Formula? 175
   What's Your Story? 176

Bibliography 179

About the Author 181

PART ONE

CHAPTER ONE

The Nail in the Neck—Got to Go through It

I rushed into the trauma bay, prepared for chaotic battle, but the bay was empty. A nurse stocked supplies. The melody of his whistle echoed through the open room.

"Where's the emergency? They called about a penetrating neck wound."

The nurse smirked and pointed to down the hallway to four cubicles separated by curtains. "He's been there for a while."

Why would anyone with a neck injury be placed in an out-of-the-way corner of an emergency room?

I tugged back the drape.

A man in his thirties sat on the edge of a hospital bed. Eyes fixed on a cell phone, he nudged the woman in the chair beside him. "Another doctor."

She wiped tears from her eyes.

"I'm Dr. Chuck. You must be Frank."

Frank looked up, frowned, and didn't reach for my offered handshake.

The woman shook my hand. "I'm Nora, Frank's wife. Please, forgive his frustration. We've been here six hours, and you're the third doctor we've seen. No one wants to fix our problem. Everyone passes us by."

Frank huffed. He pointed to the blood-stained dressing on the other side of his neck and asked, "Are you the guy who's going to pull out this nail? Everyone else is scared to do it."

Nora blew into her tissue and pointed to two black circles inked on the gauze. "Every couple of hours, the nurse comes by and draws another circle around the bloodstain. It's getting bigger. Look at the pen marks."

I peeled away the dressing, careful not to jostle the nail. The embedded metal pulsed up and down in rhythm with his heartbeat. I grabbed the nail head and prepared to jerk it out.

Frank squinted his eyes and gritted his teeth. "How bad will this hurt?"

Something made me hesitate. "How did this happen?"

Frank exhaled. "We're remodeling our garage. My wife handed me a nail gun, and it fired by accident." Frank squeezed his wife's hand and chuckled. "I knew she had it in for me."

"How long is the nail?"

Nora's voice trembled. "One inch."

I excused myself, went to the radiology suite, and reviewed the Computed Tomography (CT) scan. The nail, nestled between Frank's carotid artery and jugular vein, appeared to have missed the vital structures. The radiologist's report showed the vessels to be free from injury.

Should I pull the nail in the emergency room or get him into surgery? Unlike my predecessors, I couldn't defer the decision. The burden to decide which option would provide the best result rested on my shoulders.

Pulling the nail out in the emergency room created two possibilities. First, I could get lucky, and nothing would happen. Frank would be healthy, patched up quickly, and free to go home. The second option made me shiver. If the nail did nick a vessel, blood would quickly accumulate, restrict his airway, and create a catastrophe.

Instead of pulling the nail in the emergency room, I could take Frank to surgery, examine the injury, and investigate the status of the blood vessels. Surgery involved a much lower risk, especially if a vessel had been compromised.

When Frank moved onto the operating table, he rolled his eyes. "I knew it. I should have pulled it out at home. I want it when you're done."

I watched the anesthetist push white liquid through his IV and slide a tube down Frank's throat. The CT showed no evidence of bleeding or injury. Maybe we could have pulled it out in the ER. Had I overreacted? In any case, I had already set my course and pushed off into the unknown. Turning back was no longer an option.

I made the incision, removed the nail, and exposed the jugular vein. The nail had nicked the top of the vessel. I quickly sutured the hole closed, smiled behind my mask, and looked at the scrub tech. "Well, that was an easy fix."

THE NAIL IN THE NECK—GOT TO GO THROUGH IT

Dark blood oozed from behind the jugular. "Spoke too soon. The nail must have traveled straight through the vein. We have a hole on the backside." I compressed the vein to slow the bleed.

Stitching the top hole had been simple. Exposing the underside of a bleeding vein in a hostile situation posed a significant problem. I'd need to dissect the thin-walled vein—thinner than tissue paper—without ripping it in the process. My silent surgery team waited.

"This situation needs a little time, patience, and prayer," I said. "I'm going to hold pressure for five minutes and see if the bleeding stops on its own." I paused, trying to relieve the tension in the room. "Does anyone have a joke?"

I peered over the blue drape. Bob, the anesthetist, scanned monitors, recording data on a piece of paper.

"Bob, we need to prepare for some audible bleeding. Do we have a crossmatch ready to go?"

"Yep. I'm all over it. Already sent the request." Bob stared at a screen and cringed. "We have a small problem. We have a match, but they said it may be a couple of hours before the blood is ready."

"Get *them* on the phone and tell *them* that *they* may have to deliver blood to the morgue if it doesn't come quickly."

Bob peered over the drape. "I feel your pain. Here's a joke for you, Dr. Chuck. Do you know what we call this drape between us?"

"That gag has been around for a century."

Undeterred, Bob continued. "This sheet is the blood-brain barrier. Blood is on your side and the brains are on mine."

"How original. Here's the problem. We may need blood for this operation."

Alicia, the circulating nurse, put in her two bits. "Hey, Doc. Do you know how many surgeons it takes to screw in a light bulb?" She raised one hand and pointed to the ceiling like the Statue of Liberty. "One. The surgeon puts the bulb in the socket and expects the whole world to revolve around him."

I sighed and shook my head. "Alicia, I resemble that statement."

I held steady pressure on the vein and considered my choices. Convinced five minutes must have passed, I checked the clock. Only three. I placed the surgical tech's finger on the jugular.

"Hold gentle pressure here." I removed my hand. With his other hand, the tech gave me a thumbs up. After watching him hold the vein, I folded my arms and stepped back.

"Do you have kids?"

The surgical tech nodded; his eyes remained focused on the vein.

I stretched my neck. "My wife, Joanna, loves telling bedtime stories. Her favorite is *We're Going on a Bear Hunt*. The family encounters obstacles. High grass. Mud. A forest. A snowstorm. And with each challenge, they realize they can't get around, under, or over the obstacle. In each case, they must go through it." I chuckled. "Maybe every surgeon should read the bear hunt story. What a lesson in overcoming adversity."

I stepped back to the table and examined Frank's jugular. When I asked the scrub tech to remove his finger, blood pooled again, welling up from behind the vein.

"Uh-oh. We've awakened an angry bear."

While thoughts of bears and nails bounced around in my head, it dawned on me. I could go *through* the vein to fix the hole.

I clamped the jugular above and below the injury to stop blood flow through the vessel. I removed my previous sutures and made a larger incision on the top of the vein.

With the vessel clamped and empty of blood, I could see the injury on the backside. I sutured the tear from the inside, then re-closed the top incision. When I released the clamps, the bleeding did not resume.

"Whew. We had to go through it."

While I closed Frank's neck incision, several questions raced through my mind.

- What if Frank had pulled out the nail in his garage?
- What if I had yanked out the nail in the emergency room?
- What if I had trusted the results of the CT scan?
- What if I had damaged Frank's jugular and had torn a massive hole in the vessel?

After surgery, I planned to deliver the nail to Frank, but the nurses intervened. Policies and procedures must be followed.

When I told Frank the hospital wouldn't give him back his nail, he exploded. "What?"

I watched the staples swell over his incision and worried he would rip out the sutures on his jugular.

His face reddened. "It's my nail. I'm going to sue the hospital."

Frank's ranting didn't help him get what he wanted. He left the hospital two days later—without his nail.

We're Going on a Journey
Part One presents the first two levels of thinking. These mindsets describe the ways people see themselves, life, and the world. We can define worldview in several ways.

- A framework through which people evaluate facts, feelings, and faith.
- A set of lenses through which individuals interpret circumstances.
- A mental formula composed of various terms and factors.

Each level of thinking builds upon its predecessor, adds new elements to the mental framework, and interprets reality through a unique perspective.

First-level thinkers view situations through victim lenses, minimizing their role in changing life's outcomes. These individuals fail to recognize their own responsibility. They adopt a passive approach to life and often defer to others.

Second-level thinkers are keenly aware of their roles. They believe their responses make a difference. Strong moral feelings remind them that their life choices matter. These individuals place responsibility on themselves, believing they alone can change life's outcomes.

A Peek into Part Two
Part Two of this book presents a third level of thought. This higher way of thinking adds another factor to the mental formula—a spiritual dimension.

This level doesn't abolish the previous ones. It completes them. This mindset fulfills the others through a marriage of natural and supernatural elements, helping individuals consider life from a higher perspective. This third level achieves something its predecessors cannot: it helps us meet life's challenges with a power greater than self.

Part Two builds a framework to explain the rationale for a higher power.

This framework embraces an all-powerful Being—a God who does what we cannot do for ourselves—without minimizing personal responsibility.

This book aims to encourage all readers, regardless of religious belief. So, if you're willing, let's get started on our journey.

The Embedded Nail in Our Thinking
Everyone in the story saw Frank's circumstance from a unique perspective, and each viewpoint filtered events in different ways.

I want to introduce another *nail*, one embedded in our minds. This nail involves how we see ourselves, the world, and spirituality. How we approach it determines our life's outcomes.

Some approach their nails based on feelings. Tired and frustrated, Frank wanted to go home. He had no preference regarding the approach; he simply wanted the nail removed. With a mind clouded by impatience, he cared little about the consequences.

This thought process can be dangerous. If we don't think through options, filter facts, and consider the consequences, we may make things worse.

Others see situations based solely on facts. Downplaying emotions, they focus on cold, hard data. Another group approaches the nail solely through faith, convinced believing something makes it true.

I want to introduce you to something beyond facts, faith, and feelings: a framework for thinking to help you fit all these together.

Most people never consider how to approach the nail. They leave it alone. Avoidance may be the worst approach. We can't skirt around the nail, and we can't go over or under it.

I encourage you to go through it. Examine your mental framework.

Frank's case forced me to see things differently—to dig deeper. I had to work through a mental process, examine the evidence, and question assumptions. I'm glad I did.

Many people never consider their perspective, don't examine the filter through which they interpret life, and never question whether their assumptions fit reality.

The Fame, Blame, and Shame Game

Surgeons live and die by their choices—and so do their patients. Sometimes I'm the hero. I work through a mental process and muster an adequate response. In Frank's case, things worked out.

Sometimes my responses are inadequate. I pull out the proverbial nail and things fall to pieces. In these situations, my confidence wanes. I second-guess myself and become discouraged, wondering if a different approach would have changed the outcome.

At times, I feel like a victim in a challenging situation beyond my control when the outcome is placed in the hands of others. People point fingers at me, and sometimes I point a finger back, blaming someone else for their poor choices.

My Point of View

How can we experience life to the fullest—moving past ineffective mindsets—and see things through a different set of lenses?

The stories in this book are intended to challenge your thinking and encourage you to reassess your approach to life. I see life through the following lens: I'm a Christ-follower, and I welcome those who don't share my beliefs.

Don't accept my views at face value. Look at each chapter as a spoonful of reality, each dose opening itself to verification. Before taking medication, people should know what they're swallowing. If you're skeptical of Christianity, this book will help you understand why many people adopt this level of thinking.

Many skeptics reject Christianity without examining the evidence. Chapters eight and nine unpack the rationale for a third level of thought, giving valid reasons to believe in a God of generosity.

An inconsistent message about the Christian experience—not lack of evidence—causes confusion for most individuals. Chapter nine dispels some of these misunderstandings and explains how grace defines a third-level thinker.

This book also provides helpful tools to help Christians articulate beliefs. These principles can help you express your beliefs to a culture unfamiliar with reason, absolutes, and reality. This book aims to open conversations between those who hold a Christian worldview and those who don't.

I'm not a philosopher, a theologian, or a mathematician. I'm a surgeon. I pull nails out of people's necks. But speaking of math, I want to introduce a set of equations: each formula describes one of three levels of thinking.

The first two equations have been around for a long time. I first heard of them from Jack Canfield, author of the *Chicken Soup for the Soul* series. Apparently, he got them from Urban Meyer, and Coach Meyer gleaned them from other sources. His book, *Above the Line*, uses these formulas and presents many life-changing principles.

Both authors give valuable insight into human nature, life, and self-motivation. They clarify why many people see themselves as victims, heroes, and zeroes.

While I studied their equations, I noticed a missing element. When we add this factor into our thinking, everything changes. To my knowledge, this addition to the work done by Meyer, Canfield, and others hasn't been previously presented. I call it the life equation.

This equation doesn't undo its predecessors—it builds on them. I'm honored and humbled to share it with you.

The unexamined life is not worth living.

Socrates

CHAPTER TWO

Choices and Consequences

Hector lay on the exam table, draped his foot over the bed, and rubbed his knee. "Can you help me?"

"We'll see." I surveyed the stack of papers in his hand.

Hector removed his sock, displaying a mottled toe. "See? My toes are turning purple. And my calf hurts when I walk."

I pressed on the cold skin of Hector's toe. It turned white. "When you push on the toe, it should turn pink again, which is a sign of good blood flow. Yours doesn't. This means your capillary refill is sluggish."

I hunted for pulses in Hector's foot but found no bounding vessels.

"I'll bet you sleep better when you hang your foot over the bed."

Hector smiled. "How did you know, Doctor?"

"It's a typical complaint from people who have blockages in the blood vessels going down the leg. You have a classic presentation." I examined the pulses in Hector's groin. "Is the pain better when you rest and worse when you walk?"

Hector squinted curiously. "It was, but now my calf hurts, even when I don't walk."

I examined the yellow stains on Hector's fingers and eyed the rectangular bulge in his shirt pocket.

"How long have you been a smoker?"

"About forty years," said Hector.

"Can I have a cigarette?"

Hector reached into his pocket. "Do you smoke?"

"No, I just want to show you something. Did you know smoking causes plaque to build up in your arteries? Not just in your legs, but in your heart and brain." I held the cigarette up for him to see. "Fixing your legs and improving your health begins with a decision. You should let go of your tobacco."

Hector slapped his hand on his chest. "All I need is a good doctor to fix the blockages."

I placed the cigarette between his toes. "Sir, you need make a choice. We can do surgery, but unless you take responsibility and kick the habit, all the procedures in the world won't help."

Hector stared at the cigarette lodged between his toes.

I explained the invasive procedures he would need to restore circulation. "We first need to inject dye into your arteries. Have you ever had an arteriogram?"

Tears trickled down Hector's cheeks. He pulled the cigarette from between his toes and put it back in his shirt pocket. He slammed his stack of papers on the exam table. "I didn't come for a sermon. I thought you could help."

Looking back, I wonder if I could have approached Hector's problem with more kindness. Perhaps I was too direct, but Hector needed a strong dose of reality. Although he didn't want to hear it, he needed to realize how smoking contributed to his problems.

Hector had a choice. Since most of his condition was self-induced, he could choose a different course.

Hector's *fix my problem* mindset placed the responsibility solely on me. While medicine could help, it only would benefit Hector to a point. Unless he changed, his smoking would affect another part of his body. I needed Hector to meet me halfway by deciding to make healthy choices.

The Victim Equation

Hector's mindset is an excellent example of the first level of thinking:

$$C = O$$

C stands for life's circumstances.

- Challenges we encounter.
- Perplexing issues we face in life.

- Complex events we face on our journey.
- Obstacles which cause stress, worry, and regret.

O represents the outcome.

- The conclusion or result.
- The endpoint.

In the first level of thinking, C and O are directly proportional. In other words, if circumstances change, outcomes change as well.

In Hector's circumstance, he wanted to improve the circulation in his legs to have the outcome of pain-free living. Unaware, or perhaps unwilling, he refused to make changes which would make living without pain possible. Hector believed changing the circumstances would change his life, and he expected me to take full responsibility. Hector left the office blaming me for not fixing his outcome.

When we function this way, expecting a hero to sweep in, we look through a victim's lens.

The Victim Mindset
The victim mentality expresses itself in many ways. $C = O$ focuses on modifying C by changing something—a new job, spouse, church, location, or lifestyle. Victims expect others to step in and change things, or they leave it up to fate.

While changing circumstances can affect an outcome, victims often fail to consider what they need most: a new attitude which embraces personal responsibility.

First-level thoughts can sound like this:

- "My life is a mess because I had no opportunity."
- "I relate to others this way due to my environment. My father was an alcoholic."
- "I am angry and resentful because I was bullied as a child."
- "I could have made an A on the test, but I had no time to prepare."
- "Life would have been great, but my partner abandoned me."

Victims expect others to do for them that which they should do for themselves. Although others may play a role, victims believe other people should carry the burden.

I Am No Exception
Many years ago, I considered a career move. My surgical practice faced many obstacles, and I wasn't happy. A hospital from a larger town recruited me, promising a better opportunity than my current situation. I asked my friend Sam for advice.

Sam, a chiropractor for thirty years, had endured many life challenges, including the death of his teenage daughter.

While I dumped my list of problems on him, Sam nodded a lot and said little. After graciously listening to my complaints, Sam grabbed my hand.

"Here's something I've learned the hard way." He paused to make sure he had my attention, then whispered, "Dr. Chuck, wherever you go, there you are."

Sam intended to remind me changing my situation wouldn't solve *all* my problems. His encouragement to look inward and consider my challenges from a different viewpoint was simple but profound.

I had heard the adage before but had never grasped the full meaning. I thanked Sam for his time and left.

Without much thought, I decided to make the change and moved to the bigger town. After relocating, I began to see the wisdom of Sam's remarks. I had traded one set of problems for another.

My attempt to change my circumstances didn't produce the outcome I anticipated. I needed something more than a geographic change. I needed to change on the inside. I needed to transform my thinking.

Brandy the Bander
People who have weight-loss procedures possess distinct personalities. *Sleevers* have their procedure, move on, and seldom return to the office. *Banders*, who choose Lap-Band® surgery, are more complicated. They enjoy tweaking things and often come by for check-ups.

BRANDY THE BANDER

Brandy had her band placed several years before seeing me. On her first visit to the office, she took a selfie and posted it to her Facebook page.

"I know you didn't put in my band, but can you fill it up a little?"

Before I could answer, her phone vibrated. She looked at the screen and silenced the ringer without missing a beat.

"My twenty-year high school reunion is in two months, and I want to look my best. Can you inflate my band just a little bit?"

I examined Brandy while she *liked* responses online. Her exam revealed she had lost a significant amount of weight. Her diabetes, sleep apnea, and hypertension had resolved. She was healthier and able to exercise.

I placed my hand over her phone screen to get her attention. "Brandy, you're doing great. I recommend you stop focusing on your weight and keep making positive lifestyle changes."

Brandy smiled. "What? Just put in another half a milliliter of fluid. That's all I need."

Against my better judgment, I injected a small amount of saline into her port. The extra fluid would expand the band, tighten the stomach, and prevent overeating. Brandy left happy, ready to see old friends. Before her reunion, she returned for another adjustment.

"Doctor, I feel great. Can you let out a little fluid? I'm having some regurgitation and trouble swallowing."

In two months, Brandy had dropped thirty pounds. Her face had lost its smooth lines, and her temples curved inward. She looked like a bag of bones wrapped with flesh. She winced when I stuck the needle through her skin and into her port.

"Brandy, when is your high school get-together?"

While I withdrew saline from her port, she said. "It's this weekend. I want to be able to enjoy eating."

After loosening the band's grip on her stomach, I removed the needle.

"Dr. Chuck, how much did you remove?"

"About a milliliter."

"Thanks. See you next time." Brandy gave me a thumbs up, took another selfie, and bolted out the door.

Three months later she returned, twenty pounds heavier. I gave her a fist bump.

"Brandy, you look healthy. You're at the perfect weight."

She shook her head. "No, I'm not. I'm fat. I need to lose twenty more pounds. I'm going on a cruise with some friends."

I watched Brandy text her friends before she placed her cell phone in her purse.

She pointed to her tummy. "Just give me half a milliliter. That's all I need."

I turned the chart over and handed her a blank piece of paper. "Brandy, draw a picture of yourself."

She cocked her head, shrugged, and took the pen. After a few interrupting texts, she handed the chart back to me. Her sketch showed a distorted image, three times larger than she appeared.

I pointed to the spare tire she had drawn around her abdomen. "Brandy, why did you draw yourself to be fat? You're not obese anymore."

"It's how I see myself. Please, I need just a wee bit of fluid in my band."

Brandy had a deeper problem, one which would never be satisfied with a million lap band adjustments. Her issue, rooted in the way she saw herself, could not be fixed by me, nor by the surgeon who placed her lap band, nor by the next doctor in line.

Everyone feels like a victim at some point.

- We think changing our circumstances will fix the outcome.
- We place the burden on others to change things for us.
- In the worst case, we leave everything to fate.

On the first level of thought, C and O are the only two elements in the equation. They are directly proportional. In other words, if circumstances change, the outcome must also change.

Most people realize missing terms can be added to our mental formula. $C = O$ is only a jumping-off point.

Hector and Brandy shared something in common. They knew change was necessary, yet they failed to recognize a personal role in the process. Both placed the responsibility on someone else. When I considered moving my practice, I had the same mentality. More than anything, I needed an internal change. We were all missing something.

Before we add a missing ingredient and move to a higher level of thinking, let's expand the way we see our circumstances.

---

*Even in the valley
of the shadow of death,
two and two do not make six.*

Leo Tolstoy

CHAPTER THREE

Who Wears the Boots?

From birth, Tonya faced a unique set of challenges. Tonya was born a hermaphrodite—a genetic female having male parts. Early in life, Tonya underwent multiple surgeries to replace ambiguous parts with female anatomy.

Now, fifty years later, she had developed cancer in her reconstructed female organs.

Before Tonya's visit, a woman approached me.

"Hi, I'm Anne, with Adult Protective Services. Do you have some time to talk about Tonya after her appointment?"

I nodded. Tonya walked down the hallway, barking obscenities at my nurse, Sheila.

Sheila led her into the exam room but didn't follow her in. "I'm not going in there alone. She's more than crazy. I'm afraid she'll attack me."

"Ah," I said, "Tonya's lived a tough life, and it's about to get tougher."

I grabbed her chart and reviewed the biopsy reports. I pushed through the door to the exam room, but the odor made me step back. I regained composure and offered a handshake. Instead of taking my hand, Tonya combed her fingers through her greasy red hair.

I retracted my hand.

She snickered. "I thought about punching the cancer doctor you sent me to."

"Why?"

"He didn't look at me. He came into the room, stared at the floor, and stayed maybe for thirty seconds."

"Hmm. And what did the oncologist tell you?"

Tonya scoffed. "He told me to find another doctor. He said I need to find a specialty hospital. My case was too complicated for him. I'm not going anywhere else."

"You should consider other choices," Sheila said.

"How about MD Anderson's team?" I asked.

Tonya's lips quivered. "I'd rather die. They killed my grandmother. She got cancer. They opened her up and then zipped her closed and let her die."

"How old were you when she died, Tonya?" I asked.

"Twelve. My mother abandoned me at birth and my dad died when I was two. Grandma was the only one who wanted me. With Grandma, I felt loved and protected. If she had picked another hospital, maybe she would have lived."

"Where did you live after your grandma died?" Sheila asked.

"I went through several foster families. I was passed around by men, beaten, and raped. And when the men saw my surgery scars, they called me a misfit."

"Tonya," I said, "you have gynecological cancer. You need to be cared for by a specialist. That's why I'm referring you to a team experienced with these types of operations."

"You're trying to get rid of me. Why doesn't anyone help me?" Tonya buried her face in her hands. "All my life, everyone has been against me. Kids bullied me in elementary school. The teacher didn't let me play with the other girls. It wasn't fair."

We left Tonya's room. Sheila exhaled. "I wonder whether she will visit the referring team."

Who could tell? I headed for the next door. Before I could grab the chart, a voice interrupted.

"Doctor, I need to speak with you. Remember? I'm Anne, with Adult Protective Services."

"Oh, you're here about Tonya."

"Yes. I visited her home this week. She doesn't have running water or electricity. She never bathes, and her bathroom is a bucket." Anne sighed. "I've sent out home health nurses and every kind of service imaginable. She screams and threatens them and runs them off."

"She's a tragic case. I don't know how to help her. I don't even know where to start. How can I help you?"

Anne tapped her clipboard. "Is she competent to make decisions for herself?"

I considered before answering. "Yes. She's competent and fully aware of what she's doing. She's doing the best she knows how to do."

Anne nodded. "I'm not sure she should be living on her own, but the alternatives are just as scary. If I deem her incompetent and place her in a nursing home, she might injure and abuse others. I'm not sure what's best. Do you think she'll show up for her appointment?"

"I don't think she *wants* to go to her appointment. And if she does, I don't know how she'll get there. Nobody will take her."

Sheila cleared her throat. "You can't help those who are unwilling to help themselves. And you can't help people who don't want your help."

The Sum of Our Experiences

As in Tonya's case, many struggles are beyond our control. And often, we face a variety of life events. Using the following equation to categorize events helps us process them.

$$C = Co + Cy + Cx$$

This expression may seem intimidating at first glance, but hear me out. Circumstances have three primary sources:

Co represents the challenges we experience due to others.
Cy represents the circumstances we bring upon ourselves by our choices.
Cx represents the events which occur without explanation.

Tonya's life models all three.

Tonya's *Co* filled her life with pain. Rape. Abandonment. All kinds of physical and emotional abuse.

Tonya's *Cy* was self-induced. Her poor choices aggravated her situation. She was mean and pushed away those trying to help. She blamed others—like her grandmother's doctors—for things they couldn't control.

Tonya's *Cx* was the most perplexing. The incidence of ambiguous genitalia occurs in 0.1% of births, and cancer in those reconstructed organs is extremely rare. She also experienced deep grief over the loss of loved ones and had no support to guide her through her challenges.

Overwhelming Emotions
Most of Tonya's decisions were driven by her feelings. She possessed an *everyone's against me* attitude.

- Tonya felt she was the only person on the planet suffering adversity.
- She felt abandoned, abused, and alone.
- She felt powerless to change her circumstances.

Emotions have their place. Tonya's feelings couldn't be dismissed. They were real. We cannot ignore feelings—our own or someone else's.

Anne, Sheila, and I saw Tonya's circumstances differently. We saw them through another set of lenses:

- The facts suggested the world wasn't against Tonya. People and resources were available.
- As she worked with her new medical team, Tonya would soon realize others had faced similar challenges.
- Tonya had the power to choose, beginning with letting others help her.
- Although Tonya had been abandoned and abused in the past, she wasn't alone.

Evaluating circumstances goes deeper than facts or feelings. Our worldview is like a formula or mental gear running in our brain. It provides a filter to process our feelings—a set of lenses to help us view our reality. It's the framework to construct our view of life, and an equation to help us evaluate life events.

If Tonya changed her way of thinking, she might view her struggles differently. $C = O$, her predominant formula, did not provide the tools she needed to cope and respond in healthy ways to her struggles.

She could step into the next level by evaluating *Co*, *Cy*, and *Cx*.

- *Co*: The bullying and abuse were wrong but were in the past. These unfortunate events did not have to define her future.
- *Cy*: Tonya could evaluate her responses and become aware of how her choices complicated her situation.
- *Cx*: She could choose to accept events she couldn't explain. Her struggles were part of her history, but she could derive her identity and value from a deeper source.

Humans possess a unique quality—the power to choose. This ability comes from a higher level than a set of neurological reflexes.

Tonya forgot to employ her best asset: the power to think, decide, and grow in awareness. Victims let others choose who they are, why they exist, and how they should move forward. When we adopt a passive attitude, defer decisions to others, and let them choose our destiny, our circumstances become a decision of indecision.

Let's take a moment to think about our lives. How often do we hand off decisions to others? Does this habit affect our outcomes?

Sinking into the Victim Mindset
Success had come easily for Nathan, a wealthy real estate investor.

Three years before we met, Nathan lost Selena, his wife of thirty years, in a car accident. Nathan was devastated by Selena's absence. His confidence waned. His self-doubt grew after he lost money on a land investment. He sold his properties, took his losses, and hired others to continue his business.

We became friends when Nathan came to the office for a minor surgery. During his procedure, he shared how Selena's death had affected him. "I'm in a mental fog. I can't think straight. I wish somebody would take over."

I sent Nathan back to his primary physician, who started him on medication for depression.

Some time later, Nathan returned to the office concerned with bumps on his skin. He wore a bolo tie and new boots. For the first time since I had known him, he wore a smile. He also wore something else—a new wedding band.

"Dr. Chuck, this is Nelda."

Nelda stroked Nathan's hand and grinned. "We met online."

Noticing a twinkle in Nathan's eye, I wondered whether the change came from his new medication, his new relationship, or both.

"I'm so happy for you," I said, examining his skin. Nathan had several small flakes of sloughing skin on his face. "These lesions look like Actinic Keratosis. Nothing to worry about. We'll freeze them and schedule a follow-up."

I reached into the cabinet to grab the freeze gun, but Nelda interrupted.

"Now, wait a minute. Are you sure these aren't cancerous? And are you sure they won't come back?"

Nathan squeezed Nelda's hand. "She's the boss now, Doc."

"Yes, I'm sure. These lesions aren't cancer, but they can come back. In your husband's case, there's no benefit to cutting them off."

Nathan shrugged and looked up at Nelda, who stood beside his chair. "What do you think, sweetheart?"

"Honey, I think we need a second opinion. You're precious to me."

"Well, either way, it won't hurt me a bit," I said. "Cutting these things off will hurt you more than freezing them. And in the long run, there's little benefit."

"We'll think about it." Nelda tugged Nathan out of the chair.

I thought about how Nathan had changed. Once a confident, self-assured entrepreneur, Nathan had morphed into a hen-pecked husband. He no longer wore the boots in the family. I accepted their decision and watched the lovebirds stroll down the hallway.

A year later, I was called to the hospital to see Nathan. He was suffering from a straightforward case of diverticulitis. His children and people dressed in expensive suits crowded around his door.

A man wearing a three-hundred-dollar tie stood in my path. "Doctor, I'm the lawyer for the kids in this case. Can pain medications affect someone's state of mind and alter their ability to make sound decisions?"

"Well, of course, they can." I wondered where our conversation was headed.

The oldest son chimed in. "Doctor, this morning, Dad reversed his prenuptial agreement. Nelda has power of attorney and controls his assets."

I entered Nathan's room, where Nelda stood at his bed, rubbing his feet. A man in a dark suit wearing a four-hundred-dollar tie sat in the corner. I examined Nathan and explained my findings. "I think your inflamed colon will improve with medical treatment. At present, there's no need for surgery."

Nathan pointed to Nelda. "Ask Selena. She knows what's best."

Nelda, apparently furious at being called Selena, closed her eyes and exhaled. "Are you sure?"

"At the present, yes. I believe holding off on an operation is the best course. Let's watch him."

Before retreating and dismissing myself, I nodded at Nelda. "As always, you are welcome to get a second opinion."

Nathan, grieving the death of his first wife, had ceded responsibility to his new wife. Now, with Nelda holding the reins, Nathan experienced strained family relationships and legal battles. Losing a spouse may be one of the most difficult life events someone faces. Still, it was clear that overwhelming feelings of loneliness had muddied his mind.

Nathan had wished for someone to take over, and he got what he asked for. Nelda made choices for him. In the process, Nathan inherited a new set of challenges.

He could have stepped into the next level by evaluating *Co, Cy,* and *Cx* in this way:

- *Co*: Although Selena was taken from him, Nathan didn't need to escape with passivity. This decision created more problems than it solved.
- *Cy*: Nathan could have evaluated his responses to become aware of how his choices complicated the situation.
- *Cx*: Nathan could have sought help to accept the events he couldn't explain.

Trapped in the Analysis Paralysis

Circumstances are seldom simple. Life challenges are a collage of feelings and facts, things in our control, and experiences we can't change. Often, we feel as though life events have trapped us in a cage of despair.

Remember, circumstances have three primary sources.

Co: Challenges we experience due to others.

- Can we name ours?

Cy: Circumstances we bring upon ourselves by our choices.

- Can we see ours?

Cx: Events which occur without explanation.

- Can we define ours?

Framing our challenges is a necessary exercise but is not the end goal. Evaluating things with the C equation begins the process of transformation.

Tonya and Nathan both suffered emotional scars—ones which may never heal. Like them, everyone faces circumstances impossible to get over. We need to get through them. But how?

One flaw in victim thinking comes from the inability to correct things which have already occurred. These circumstances can't be controlled or changed. $C = O$ thinking doesn't empower us to move forward. Instead, first-level thinking fixates on life's problems without providing tools to manage them.

Consider the following questions:

- How much attention do we spend on our life challenges?
- How much do we focus on seeing the opportunities our adversity brings?

In the next chapter, we'll explore the next level of thinking. We'll add another element to the equation, one which gives us the power to change. Adding this new term helps us see opportunities within obstacles.

The whole of society is seen to be subject to the interplay of clashing forces, sometimes balancing, and sometimes dominating one another. It is like an infinite series of equations, each expressing the inter-relationships of its members. And each of these equations is composed of many terms, positive as well as negative . . . We are not dealing with fixed, dead mathematical formulae, but with life . . .

Paul Tournier

CHAPTER FOUR

Please, Chop 'Em Off
Patient with Cerebral Palsy requests an Above Knee Amputation. I waved Garth's intake form at my nurse. "Are you sure? Nobody *wants* to have their leg removed."

Before I could get through the exam room door, Garth said, "D . . . doctor, ch . . . chop my l . . . l . . . legs off! B . . . b . . . both of th . . . them."

In my twenty years of practice, no one had ever asked for an amputation. The difficulty of amputation—a straightforward operation—usually lies in convincing patients of the need to remove an appendage. Most people feel attached to their legs.

"You he . . . hea . . . heard me. I ne . . . nee . . . need you to c . . . cut off b . . . b . . . both my l . . . l . . . legs." Garth's head jerked.

Still taken aback, I listened while Garth stammered.

"When do you h . . . have an o . . . open . . . nnn . . . ing in your schedule? Are you gonna chop them b . . . b . . . both off at once or one at a t . . . t . . . time?"

"Garth, why do you want an amputation?"

Garth shook his head uncontrollably. "M . . . my legs h . . . hold me b . . . ba . . . ack."

I removed his shoes, lifted his pant leg, and suddenly understood Garth's predicament. His toothpick legs were locked at the knees. Weeping sores covered his feet and lower legs.

I looked up at Garth. One blue eye peered straight at me while the other focused on the wall. "How long have you had these flexion contractures of your knees?"

"For at least t . . . tw . . . twe . . . wenty years," Garth garbled, "I s . . . suffered from b . . . b . . . birth c . . . c . . . complic . . . cations. C . . . cereb . . . bral P . . . p . . . palsy."

Garth's family lived deep in the Texas Pineywoods with little money and no access to resources. Garth was born fifty years ago, before much was known about Cerebral Palsy. People assumed individuals with CP also had an intellectual disability. Embarrassed by his son, Garth's alcoholic father hid him away.

"When c . . . com . . . comp . . . company came, they s . . . sh . . . shut me up in my r . . . r . . . room. Once, my da . . . dad . . . daddy sent me away to s . . . s . . . school. He wanted to g . . . get rid of me. Bu . . . but I sh . . . showed them."

Garth's response to his challenges was inspiring. Anyone who saw past his speech impediment and uncontrollable movements found an intelligent, articulate, and perceptive individual.

"When I was yo . . . young, f . . . frie . . . friends said, 'P . . . po . . . poor little G . . . Ga . . . Garthy.' But I would te . . . tell them, 'D . . . don't fe . . . feel s . . . s . . . sorry for m . . . me. I'm f . . . f . . . fine.'"

Despite his father's opposition, Garth learned a trade and married. He never let his physical challenges keep him from doing all the things he could do. Though Garth was disabled, isolated, disadvantaged, and misunderstood, those roadblocks never entered his mind. He wouldn't accept the pity of others.

People with legitimate challenges have many opportunities to pull out their victim cards. When they don't, something special happens.

Garth claimed ownership of his circumstances, accepted them, and moved forward. Garth took personal responsibility.

The Second Level of Thinking

R represents response.

Garth's response to his adversity transformed the outcome of his life. Choosing to respond positively, Garth embraced the hero equation, which provides a different framework from that of $C = O$.

This formula uses $C = Co + Cy + Cx$ but shifts focus. Here's how:

- Our response to the event, rather than the event itself, becomes the focus.

THE SECOND LEVEL OF THINKING

- We see ourselves as the hero rather than the victim.
- We move from passivity to action.
- We shift from depending on others to helping ourselves.
- Instead of changing life's events, we work on changing ourselves.

When we accept responsibility, the equation becomes:

$$C + R = O$$

Responsible thinkers focus on attitudes and actions which can change outcomes. This level focuses on the present, on the possibilities which lie ahead, and on the opportunities life's obstacles bring. Hero thinkers consider ways to be resourceful and creative. They acknowledge personal responsibility, take initiative, and adjust their reactions to a situation.

In short, a victim dwells on things they cannot change and situations they can't control, while second-level thinkers focus on what they can change and what they can control.

Differentiating between Co, Cy, and Cx becomes very important to heroes. Aware they can't change what others do or have done to them, heroes don't waste time pondering the imponderables. They take control through their attitudes and actions. They work to decrease the number of negative situations which they bring upon themselves.

Level	Equation	Focus	Responsibility
First	$C = O$	Circumstances	Someone Else
Second	$C + R = O$	Responses	Self

The $C + R = O$ formula draws on self-awareness, self-sufficiency, and self-effort. Viktor Frankl, a neurologist who survived a Nazi concentration camp, modeled this attitude. In Auschwitz, Germans took everything away from Frankl—his loved ones, his health, his personal dignity, and his basic physical needs of life.

During Frankl's loss and suffering, he clung to something the Nazis couldn't take away: his ability to choose. Through his tragedies, Frankl realized he could decide how to respond to his challenges. Frankl experienced a new sense of freedom.

"When we are no longer able to change a situation, we are challenged to change ourselves." Frankl and many others have championed this second level of thinking.

A Hero in the Strife
My seventh-grade teacher required our class to memorize and recite *A Psalm of Life*. For weeks, I practiced the stanzas. Trembling, I stood before the class and quoted the words of Longfellow.

> *In the world's broad field of battle,*
> *In the bivouac of Life,*
> *Be not like dumb, driven cattle!*
> *Be a hero in the strife!*
>
> *Trust no Future, howe'er pleasant!*
> *Let the dead Past bury its dead!*
> *Act, —act in the living present!*
> *Heart within, and God o'erhead!*

Longfellow's words remind us attitudes and actions determine our destiny. Heroic feats are accomplished when we concentrate on positive responses to life's obstacles. These works remind us we are the hero of the story.

The Power of Self-awareness
We possess the ability to examine ourselves, consider our motives, and enhance our performance. We can contemplate our potential, consider how to fulfill ourselves, and set a course of action.

A group traveled to learn from a Himalayan teacher. They were told this sage possessed all of life's answers. When they found the wise man, the members fought for an opportunity to ask questions and discuss their problems. After listening to hours of bickering, the monk asked them to sit in a circle, write down their problems on a piece of paper, and place them in a bowl.

The sage then passed the bowl around the circle. "Pick the top piece of paper and read the problem. Now, choose either to keep your own problem or to trade your problem for the one you read."

One by one, each traveler read everyone else's problems, placed the papers back in the bowl, and chose to accept their own circumstances.

The Power of Ingenuity

Creativity recognizes that doing the same thing in the same way produces the same results. We have the mental capacity to analyze a problem, brainstorm ideas, organize possibilities, and formulate solutions.

Creative thinkers ask questions about their challenges, observe their situations, and connect unrelated ideas. Instead of aggravating the problem, ingenuity helps heroes become part of the solution.

Leonardo da Vinci's ingenuity involved more than art. In addition to painting the Mona Lisa, he created a rolling mill, a helicopter, a parachute, a sanitation system for a city, a robot, and a war tank. He sketched the human body, providing detailed anatomical drawings of organs, bones, heart valves, and the fetus in utero.

His ability to connect unrelated things fostered creativity.

The Power of Initiative

A man hired three brothers to help on his farm. He told each of the boys to go to town and find out what goods had arrived with the morning train.

The oldest brother called the depot, talked to the train personnel, and hurried back to his boss. "One hundred head of cattle."

The youngest brother returned several hours later. "The train had one hundred cows, one thousand heads of lettuce, and some tools."

That evening, the middle brother handed the farmer a head of lettuce and a folded stack of cash. "One car had a hundred cows. I made a deal with a broker two towns up the tracks. I sold them for ten dollars more per head than I bought them for. I did the same with the lettuce."

"What about the tools?"

"No good. The hoe handles had cracks and the metal was chipped. I let them stay on the train."

The farmer told his wife, "The oldest didn't do what I asked him to do. The youngest did only what I told him. But the middle boy went above and beyond."

The farmer promoted the middle brother to supervise the youngest brother, then fired the oldest.

Second-level thinkers like the middle brother take initiative. Everyone possesses the ability to act, decide on a course, and take positive steps forward.

The Power of Resourcefulness

Resourcefulness involves finding available tools and putting them to work. Resourceful people find the strength to endure their problems and keep going.

Climbing solo in Utah, Aron Ralston faced an overwhelming obstacle in Blue John Canyon. During his descent into the canyon, a large boulder fell on Aron's hand. Alone and trapped, sixty feet up a cliff, Aron had only one option: amputation.

For three days, the climber worked to sever his hand with a multitool, ultimately breaking the bones in his forearm. He finished his descent with one hand. Fortunately, Aron was found by a family of campers, made it to the hospital, and survived.

Resourceful people adopt a *whatever it takes* attitude and face life's challenges by utilizing what they have.

The Power of Adaptability

Brent, a man in his eighties, had Alzheimer's Disease. His wife Jenny brought him back to the office one year after he had a feeding tube placed.

"This tube is cracking. It leaks when you push fluid through it. Can you replace it here in the office?" Jenny caressed her husband's hand.

She was right. When I irrigated the tube, fluid leaked through the cracks. "Why has it taken so long to follow up?" I asked.

"He's been in lockdown at the nursing home. With the COVID epidemic, no one was allowed in or out."

"And how have things been during this time, Miss Jenny?"

The aging woman wiped away a tear and sniffled. "I used to stay all day in the nursing home. During the pandemic, they shut me out for six months."

I removed the feeding tube and replaced it with a new one. I injected saline into the tube and fixed it in place. "There you go," I said.

Jenny shook her head. "That was fast and easy."

"So, Miss Jenny, how did you cope with not seeing your husband for almost half a year?"

Jenny's expression changed. She pulled down her mask and chuckled. "I cheated. I saw him every day."

"How?"

"I sat in a chair outside the nursing home by his window. I got there early in the morning and stayed all day. We could see each other through the window. My daughter set up a microphone attached to an app on my cell phone. We talked every day, just like we have for the last sixty years. When it rained, I brought my umbrella. And when it didn't rain, I brought my umbrella. You know how hot this Texas sun gets."

I left the room, amazed at Jenny's innovation. Instead of complaining about social distancing or nursing home restrictions, she adapted to her circumstances. She couldn't change the rules, and she couldn't change the pandemic. She found a creative way to work around her circumstances.

Individuals can adapt to life's obstacles. They can recognize when a course of action isn't working, adjust, and choose a different path. If an octogenarian can learn to be flexible, so can we. Miss Jenny's courageous response to the COVID pandemic expressed love for her husband.

The Power of an Unconquerable Spirit

Self-awareness, creativity, initiative, and adaptability flow out of the second level, focusing on the self's power to change.

British poet William Ernest Henley suffered from tuberculosis. Like Garth, Henley had to have an amputation. In the hospital, he penned a poem—*Invictus,* which means "unconquerable"—praising self's ability to take control and master one's destiny:

Out of the night that covers me
Black as the pit from pole to pole
I thank whatever gods may be
For my unconquerable soul.

In the fell clutch of circumstance
I have not winced or cried aloud.
Under the bludgeonings of chance,
My head is bloody, but unbowed.

Beyond this place of wrath and tears,
Looms but the horror of the shade.
And yet the menace of the years
Finds, and shall find, me unafraid.

It matters not how strait the gate
How charged with punishments the scroll
I am the master of my fate:
I am the captain of my soul.

Invictus inspires us to be the hero and believe in the power of self.

The $C + R = O$ formula reminds us we are accountable for our choices. Many life events are beyond our control, but we don't have to be defeated and powerless. How we respond to challenges will influence life's outcome.

In second-level thinking, the language shifts.

- "I made a bad decision yesterday which I can't change, but I can make better choices today."
- "I cannot change my broken past, but I may be able to transform my future."
- "I take responsibility and accept the consequences."

Accepting responsibility and embracing a positive attitude are keys to success. Second-level thought provides valuable tools to help us rise above our life events. Heroes draw on resources which victims fail to recognize. Adding the R term to the mix reminds us of accountability.

However, second-level thinking has a deep-rooted flaw. Placing humankind—or the self—as the measure of all things creates real dilemmas. Sometimes, heroes hurt others. And in bearing a hero's burdens, $C + R = O$ thinkers often wound themselves. Questions surface when we think deeply about $C + R = O$.

- To whom are we accountable?
- What determines the validity of our responses?
- Is self-effort adequate to meet all life challenges?

In the next chapter, we'll unpack some second-level weaknesses.

The price of greatness is responsibility.

Winston Churchill

CHAPTER FIVE

We Have Met the Enemy and . . .
Embracing responsibility costs something. When a person's greatness grows, they bear an increasingly heavy load of expectations. Champions with a strong reputation face more scrutiny, opposition, and difficulties.

Every hero hides a secret.

- Superman is vulnerable to Kryptonite.
- Batman possesses a dark side with a painful past.
- While saving the world, Mr. Incredible creates collateral damage.

Aware of their imperfections, strong responders know they cannot live up to the expectations of those who rely on them.

I have the utmost admiration for my surgical mentors. One was a pioneer in trauma surgery who improvised techniques, wrote books, and inspired a generation of doctors. This phenomenal teacher projected a save-the-day personality. Out of respect for his confidentiality, we'll call him Dr. Wilson.

My first week of surgical residency at Baylor College of Medicine, I was on call at Ben Taub Hospital. A green intern, I had no skills, no experience, and no judgment. My job was to wheel beds and to perform all the undesired tasks nobody wanted. I existed to help individuals higher on the surgical pyramid.

That evening, Dr. Wilson was in charge. My peers were anxious, knowing the man who controlled their surgical destiny called the shots.

Six gunshot victims were hauled in from a gang fight at two in the morning. Our team prioritized the injured, deciding which needed immediate surgery and which could wait. While my supervisors operated on the sickest patients, I received a promotion from bed pusher to babysitter. I was charged to care for a not-so-sick patient.

The chief resident barked, "He's stable. Obey the nurses and keep him alive. I'll be back."

With the help of seasoned trauma nurses, I cared for my patient. He had a gunshot wound to the lower left chest. The bullet had punctured the lung, appearing to miss the other vital organs.

I ordered a chest X-ray and began my evaluation. Out of nowhere, Dr. Wilson sprang into the room. "Why did you order a chest X-ray? You know he has a pneumothorax. You've wasted your time and a test. Place a chest tube before they take the film."

I fumbled through the procedure while Dr. Wilson peered over my shoulder. I pushed a large clamp into the patient's side. His punctured chest wall expelled a large gush of air. The patient screamed but relaxed as his breathing improved.

"See," Dr. Wilson said, "that first X-ray wouldn't have changed anything. All he needed was a chest tube. Bring me the film when it comes back." He disappeared almost as quickly as he'd arrived.

Alone again, I studied the monitor. The bullet's trajectory seemed close to the diaphragm—the muscle which separated the lungs from the abdominal organs. Could the bullet have tracked through the spleen?

When the chest X-ray returned, I found Wilson in the hallway, supervising three other gunshot victims. I showed him the X-ray.

"Sir, this patient's pulse pressure seems to be narrowed. Could the bullet have gone below the diaphragm and tracked through the spleen?"

Wilson held the X-ray up to the light and pointed to the bullet holes. "Impossible. Wheel him to the back."

Without question, I pushed the gunshot victim to a large room filled with patients waiting for tests. I carried on writing orders and checking radiology reports.

Minutes later, the chief resident rushed my patient into the trauma room. "What's wrong with you? I told you to keep him alive. Didn't it cross your mind the bullet could have hit his spleen? Get him to the OR—now!"

I wheeled the dying patient into the operating room, once again following the orders of my superiors. "Gunshot wound to the spleen. He's crashing."

The team set to work, and soon the patient was asleep, prepped, and prepared for surgery. When the chief resident opened the belly, liters of dark blood were removed.

Unknown to us, Dr. Wilson was watching over our shoulders. His deep voice echoed through the room. "What's this?"

My chief spoke up. "GSW to the chest. The bullet traversed the diaphragm and nicked his spleen. Page missed it."

Wilson chuckled under his surgical mask. Dr. Wilson led my superior through the operation, giving him pointers and demonstrating one of his famous maneuvers. Soon, the spleen was in a bucket, and the patient stabilized.

Wilson never said a word about missing the splenic injury on the X-ray. In the operating room, my hero concealed the truth, took the fame, and deflected the blame to me—the lowly intern. Perhaps it was an oversight. Perhaps the situation was too chaotic to stop and discuss the case.

What I didn't see that crazy night were the five other gunshot wounds my attending had juggled. Wilson managed chaos—and managed it well.

Heroes carry a heavy load of expectations. Greater successes lead to greater burdens. Admirers expect heroes to be omniscient, omnipresent, and omnipotent. Many strong responders place even higher expectations upon themselves.

Their degree of performance determines their acceptance. When heroes measure up, they receive approval both from others and from themselves. When they fail, they fear removal from the pedestal. To be accepted, heroes feel they must perform—or else. They live in a cycle where enough is never enough.

My experiences with heroes continued during my next surgical rotation. Several months later, I worked under Dr. Michael Ellis Debakey. He was Dr. Wilson's hero. What Dr. Wilson was to trauma, Dr. Debakey was to surgery. Even his initials—M. E. D.—implied something.

Dr. Debakey's discoveries influenced medicine in the twentieth century. His name was familiar in American households. In medical school, he developed the roller pump. This device circulated blood out of the body, allowing surgeons to repair the heart.

SPOONFUL OF COURAGE

In World War II, he masterminded M. A. S. H. hospitals. Debakey pioneered aortic surgery—the main blood vessel coming from the heart—and developed techniques to prevent strokes and heart attacks.

I bowed before the icon, placing the chart between his pencils. By accident, the chart knocked a pencil on the floor.

Debakey said, "Are you incompetent? Or do you simply not care?"

I looked behind me at the entourage of specialists and dignitaries, hoping someone would come to my rescue. They remained silent.

Embarrassed, I bowed lower and picked up the pencil, noticing Debakey's odd white shoes. Henny, his nurse, stood on his other side, placing films on the board. She distracted his attention away from me, giving me time to gather my composure.

"Show me the run-offs," he grumbled.

Henny placed every X-ray on the view board.

Dissatisfied, Debakey barked, "There's another film showing the blood vessels in the foot. Where is it?"

"Sir, don't you remember? We looked at them yesterday and you took the film with you." I said.

He poked my chest, peering up at me with his cold, black eyes. "You're lying. You lost it. Find it, or I'll hold your paycheck."

"Yes, sir."

Debakey stood and walked through a room filled with pictures of himself with celebrities and presidents. His strange white boots caused an unsteady gait. He entered his private chamber and slammed the door. When the door closed, everyone sighed, relieved.

One of the heart surgeons, famous in his own right, slapped me on the back. "Well, Chuck. It's official—you're a Baylor Boy. And that performance was one for the books." He smiled. "I saw him take the foot films, but you need to find them. Who knows where he put them. Don't worry. I'll call the office and get your paycheck."

Like Debakey, he stabbed me in the chest with his finger. "Don't sleep till you find those films."

"I've checked everywhere, sir."

The surgeon shook his head. "It's your future. Not mine."

For the third night in a row, I stayed up, rummaging around the radiology department, looking for films my mentor had misplaced.

The following morning, I assisted while the heart surgeon made an incision on a patient's neck. As other surgeons piled into the case, I was shoved farther away from the operation. Finally, I stood behind two surgeons, holding a retractor.

I briefly shut my eyes. A hard object hit me in the chest, and my eyes flew open. Debakey had punched my sternum again with his bony finger, "Boy, do you want to keep your job?"

He turned, left the room, and went to wash his hands, almost tripping in his high boots.

The anesthesiologist whispered in my ear. "Denton Cooley stands almost a foot taller than Debakey. That's why he wears high steppers."

Debakey reentered the room and donned a surgical gown displaying his M. E. D. initials. The Red Sea parted, and the legend approached the patient. He cut the neck artery open, peeled away a large plaque, and sewed the vessel closed.

Debakey tugged on my hand, forcing me to pull harder on my retractor.

"Where's the film, Page?"

"Sir, I couldn't find it." I was surprised Debakey knew my name.

"Young fella, do you know the difference between your hands and mine?" Before I could answer, he said, "It's the brain behind my hands."

He finished stitching and nodded to the team. "You boys take it from here."

Debakey walked over to the view box, rummaged through an old stack of X-rays, and pulled out the missing film. He held it up to the light. When he realized I was watching, he quickly turned and left the room, carrying the lost X-ray with him.

I almost lost my job over a trivial thing: a misplaced X-ray. The icon never acknowledged he had taken the film, and he blamed me for his forgetfulness.

At the time, I didn't understand the burden resting on my mentor's shoulders. The misplaced films were those of a foreign dignitary who ruled an entire nation. And Debakey's performance—good or bad—had far-reaching consequences. Giving up control of his high-profile patients to an untested intern like me made him suspicious and distrustful. From a hero's point of view, those films were not trivial. A lot rested on those X-rays.

Heroes like Debakey deserve our respect. We should honor their achievements. In retrospect, I learned many things from my mentor. Now, I consider it a privilege to have trained under the surgical giant.

Reflecting on those times, I now see Debakey through a different set of lenses. Having carried a similar load of burdens and expectations, I have more empathy. At times, I tried to play the hero and failed. I have hurt others by blaming them for my insufficiencies, pointing fingers of blame, and taking credit for things I shouldn't have. In the process, I have also hurt myself.

Being the hero of our own story isn't all we dress it up to be. There are downsides to $C + R = O$.

Many champions understand their leadership is essential and people depend on them, so they hide their weaknesses to protect their image.

Some heroes become angry and insecure. They live in fear their imperfections will be exposed. They distrust everyone and develop deep emotional wounds. Damaged people damage others. This is one of the great prices a hero pays. Many champions

- fear failure,
- stress about having their inadequacies exposed,
- justify their actions,
- criticize,
- blame others,
- distrust people who could help them,
- isolate themselves from intimate relationships, and
- waste time and energy focusing on self-preservation.

Strong responders who live on the performance treadmill develop an "if I don't do it, it won't get done" attitude.

The "Don't Make Me a Hero" Heroes

Some heroes take a different approach, exposing inadequacies instead of hiding them. They stand on the "don't place me on a pedestal" pedestal. You'll hear these types of heroes use phrases like

- transparent leadership,
- vulnerability,
- win-win relationships, and
- nurturing self-esteem.

They use different tools to show the sufficiency of their responses, which loosens the noose around their neck. When a negative outcome occurs, they point fingers at the process instead of the person. They aim to enhance the esteem of others, hoping to improve performance.

Although this approach may have its upsides, the noose of expectations is still looped around the hero's neck, ready to strangle. When weak responses occur, the rope tightens and chokes the hero.

Regardless of technique, the price of responsibility can't be escaped. The reality of acceptance based on performance reminds even the strongest responders—enough is never enough.

The key isn't found in new techniques or tools. A better answer begins with adding another element to the formula.

$C + R = O$ doesn't have the power to match all of life's challenges. Strong responders are never strong enough to meet every life event. Eventually, every champion fails. They cannot meet all the expectations placed on their lives. Every hero possesses a deficiency: themselves.

Who's the Enemy?

In my final years of training, I moved up the surgical hierarchy. Dr. Gene Guinn was a skillful mentor. He had the knack of making complicated procedures simple and knew how to teach young surgeons. In the middle of surgery, Dr. Guinn challenged my thinking about being a champion.

I placed a large clamp on the aorta, impeded blood flow to the legs, and opened the artery. After removing plaque from the aorta, I oversewed several bleeders on the backside of the vessel.

Dr. Guinn looked over my work. "Dry coming in. Dry going out. Attaboy."

He held a tube in one hand and pointed to the aorta. "Now take a big bite with that stitch on the outside of the aorta and place your next bite on the inside of this graft."

I obeyed while my mentor kept the suture from tangling.

"Move along. Outside in, then inside out," he said. "Did you know Debakey's mother made the first Dacron tube graft? Dacron is pretty good material. It's flexible, it's durable, and it doesn't bleed much."

I finished one side of the suture line.

"Now pull the tube graft down on the aorta and sew the top side."

My suture tangled and knotted.

"Hold on, Dr. Chuck." Dr. Guinn unraveled the suture. "Boy, remind me never to take you fishing."

I continued sewing while Dr. Guinn sighed. "We have met the enemy, and the enemy is ourselves."

Dr. Guinn's adage was self-explanatory. We can dress up our responses, but sometimes we are our own worst enemy. No matter how we optimize our performance, we can't escape ourselves. Strong responses and self-confidence will not always conquer every challenge we experience.

The Human Dilemma

We're disappointed when we fail ourselves and when others fail us. Perhaps strong and confident responders weren't made to be placed on pedestals. Could it be that we aren't heroes in the story?

Yet we long for a hero. We want to place impossible expectations—a set of universals no one can keep—on ourselves and others.

We can add another element to our thinking: one which explains why we have these expectations, one which empowers our responses, one which shifts the hero-burden off ourselves. Before we do, we need to explore another kind of second-level thinker.

Although they possess the same mental equation as heroes, they see themselves through a different set of lenses. This group—the weak responders, the zero thinkers, might be more emotionally honest than their strong counterparts.

> If I find in myself desires which nothing in this world can satisfy, the only logical explanation is that I was made for another world.

C.S. Lewis

CHAPTER SIX

The Second-level See-saw

Two kinds of people exist on the second level. The first group, heroes, see their responses as adequate. These responses project confidence, accountability, and determination.

- Find yourself.
- Be yourself.
- Dream.
- Picture yourself achieving the outcome you desire.
- Set goals for self-attainment.
- Motivate and inspire yourself.
- Modify your self-performance and, with self-effort, achieve your goals.

The second group is wired differently. Although keenly aware of their responsibility, they lack confidence and believe their responses to life events are inadequate. They see themselves as failures.

Heroes refer their counterparts to the above list. Add a little self-evaluation and self-actualization into the mix, instill a pinch of self-belief, place it in the oven of adversity, and *voila*! Out pops a self-assured champion.

Many weak responders have tried the hero recipe many times. They follow the instructions and precisely measure the ingredients, but when their masterpiece comes out of the oven, it's a disaster.

Zeroes realize life challenges aren't as simple as strong responders suggest. Intuitively, they understand an ingredient is missing, and the forgotten element isn't a new self-help technique. They search but can't find the missing element.

Joan, a mother of three, came to her physician with signs of depression. Her husband, Jose, a busy executive, provided all the material things she wanted. To those looking in from the outside, Joan appeared to have everything. Money. Good social standing. A growing family. From the inside, Joan saw the situation through a different set of lenses.

"Jose feels distant," said Joan. "We never talk anymore, and I think he may be having an affair with another woman. My world is falling apart. I can't sleep. When I lie in bed, all the things I haven't done race through my mind. I've got a week's worth of laundry sitting in a basket."

She buried her face in her hands. "And I think my teenage daughter, Sarah, is sleeping with her boyfriend."

Joan received antidepressants, a pep talk, and a follow-up appointment. The following day, she dropped the kids off at school, drove out into the woods, and took her own life.

Like so many others, Joan bore the weight of the world on her shoulders. She didn't use the victim card, make excuses, or blame anyone else for her troubles. Jan was aware of her responsibilities and felt her burdens were too much to bear on her own. In her mind, suicide became the best solution.

Unlike the first level thinkers, zero thinkers are mindful of their responses. They believe themselves to be incompetent. They try, but they can't acquire the qualities necessary to change the outcome of their lives. Tragically, like Joan, they wear a cloak of shame and guilt on their shoulders.

Weak responders don't have the strength to face life's obstacles, and they know it. They wear zero lenses, perceiving themselves as inadequate.

In their mental formula, Zeroes replace the capital R with a lowercase r, which represents an inadequate response.

The zero equation parallels its counterpart—with one difference. Zeroes see insufficiency when they evaluate their own performance. A weak responder's formula looks like this:

$$C + r = O$$

Think of the zero and hero mentalities as two sides of a coin. Same equation, but each side interprets the R/r term from a different viewpoint.

On one side, the zero thinkers see the weakness in their words, thoughts, and deeds. On the other side of the coin, heroes strive to provide assertive responses to their life challenges.

Although aware of their responsibility, the weak think they don't possess the power to change the outcome. Believing their responses are inadequate, they substitute a lower-case r.

Formula	Lenses	Response	Focus	Self-Esteem
$C + r = O$	Zero	Passive & Weak	Inadequate responses	Low
$C + R = O$	Hero	Active & Strong	Adequate responses	High

Most zeroes don't take extreme measures like Joan. They do the reverse: nothing. Weak responders live their lives in quiet desperation. They seldom take risks. They fail to believe in themselves and exhibit low self-esteem. They live paralyzed by fear, regret, and guilt.

A Shocking Story
Unlike Joan, many people don't give up. They keep going, trying to adjust their responses. They teeter-totter back and forth on a pendulum of emotions, swinging between the zero and hero formulas.

I met Wilma on my first medical school rotation in psychiatry. In her sixties, Wilma came to the hospital with symptoms of depression: insomnia, guilt, apathy, lethargy.

This sweet lady had faced some challenging obstacles.

Her husband neglected her. Wilma's son had divorced, gotten into drugs, and abandoned her grandchildren. She'd had a strained relationship with her sister, Betty, who had died of breast cancer.

Wilma fretted over the future and lived in fear of cancer. She believed she would suffer and die like her sister. "Cancer runs in families, you know."

After a trial of antidepressants failed, the psychiatry attending suggested electroconvulsive therapy (ECT). Each morning, we wheeled Wilma into a room, attached electrodes to her brain, and sedated her.

When she fell asleep, we zapped her brain with an electric current, bringing her into a convulsive state.

After two weeks of treatments, I questioned my attending. "Aren't seizures dangerous? How safe is ECT? Don't we have better ways to treat depression?"

She put her hands in her white coat pockets and shrugged. "It works."

And it did. Wilma felt better about herself and her obstacles. She stopped borrowing trouble from the future and began to see things from a different point of view. After finishing her shock treatments, Wilma went home. She seemed to feel good about herself.

Six months later, during my surgery rotations, Wilma came back to the hospital for bilateral mastectomies. Surprised to see Wilma's name on the surgery docket, I visited her in the preoperative area.

"How are you?"

Wilma looked at the wall and wiped her eyes with a tissue. "Hi, Dr. Chuck. I decided to stop worrying about this and get it done. I'm having both of my breasts removed. I'd rather die from surgery than from breast cancer."

During surgery, I asked the surgeon the rationale for removing both breasts.

"Prophylaxis." He removed Wilma's left breast.

"Did she have any abnormal findings on her studies?"

"Nope." The surgeon cut the skin on the other side.

"Any genetic abnormalities?"

The surgeon stopped and glared at me across the table. "No. A chance to cut is a chance to cure."

After we finished, the plastic surgery team reconstructed both breasts. After six hours in the operating room, Wilma was sent to the floor to recuperate.

Wilma failed to get up after surgery. Despite our team's encouragement, she lay in bed for several days, depressed.

We called in the psychiatrist who had given the shock treatments. She gave medications which heavily sedated Wilma, making her even more bed bound.

Wilma developed a blood clot in her leg, which traveled to her lungs—a pulmonary embolus.

When I visited Wilma in the intensive care unit, she moaned. "Everything I've tried has failed." Wilma's eyes filled with tears. "I'll never try anything again."

Wilma decided to act instead of fretting about the possibility of breast cancer, but the outcome of Wilma's hero response wasn't what she expected. Wilma almost lost her life, but not from cancer.

The Second Guesser's See-saw
Many people, like Wilma, see-saw on the second level. Their mental formula swings back and forth. Sometimes they are up, perceiving themselves as heroes, making decisive choices. And the next, facing another set of events, they swing down. They lose confidence and second-guess their weak responses. Some people, like Joan, swing to the bottom and remain in helpless despair.

Champions encourage the Wilmas of the world to stop waxing and waning between the two equations. For self-helpers, the solution is clear and simple. Believe in yourself—with a capital R.

Heroes encourage zeroes. "Yes, you can."

Zeroes know themselves better. "No, I can't."

Many people exist somewhere between the two mindsets, oscillating between feelings of strength and weakness.

Here are some questions to ponder:

- How do we perceive our responses?
- Are they strong or weak?
- What framework do we use to measure the validity of our responses?

Second-level Ambiguity
If we probe deeply into the second level, some questions surface. In Wilma's story, which doctor suggested the best course—the psychiatrist or the surgeon? Facts supported both courses of treatment. Many studies show

shock treatments help cure depression. Was the surgeon's approach a chance to cure or a chance to kill? Who decides?

On this level, the *self* measures responses and outcomes. Second-level thinkers suggest all humans, beginning with themselves, have the capacity to measure all things. In this framework, man does more than play in the game. The self serves as the umpire.

Imagine a baseball game in which individual players make their own rules. Was the pitch a ball, or was it a strike? A second-level answer depends upon who answers the question. Will the pitcher or the batter decide? Or should the pitcher's mother and the batter's girlfriend duke it out? To various degrees, this formula asserts that any individual may referee.

On the second level, every person seems to have a different view. Each employs facts, expresses strong feelings supporting their conclusions, and believes strongly in a viewpoint.

Who has the final authority to determine optimal responses?

In one sense, leaving responsibility to each individual gives everyone a sense of comfort. All opinions are valid. There's no need to offend anyone, no reason to confront others about their choices. Dostoevsky notes how a relativistic formula can entice us. "The formula 'two and two make five' is not without its attractions."

Yet we fail to perceive the negative: the hook hidden within the bait, the downside to a framework without absolutes. Without an external reference to judge between parties, arbitration poses real problems. At best, we're left with relativism—if it's true for the individual, it must be true.

Based on the second level, one choice appears as good as another. Without an umpire, the game devolves into chaos, and the strongest team wins.

This inherent lack of objectivity leaves us with arbitrary absolutes. The only way to settle disputes comes through power. Thus, the strong impose their will on the weak.

Starting with the self and thinking in relativistic terms, man has no universals. Without an umpire to call the game, we're left on our own to measure appropriate responses and outcomes.

SECOND-LEVEL AMBIGUITY

As we'll see in upcoming chapters, the third level of thought employs a different set of intellectual assumptions, ones without duplicity.

- Self is not sufficient to measure responses and outcomes on their own.
- Absolutes exist outside of man and external to the self.
- Man isn't the ultimate source for understanding life and the universe.

Third-level thinkers believe something is missing in the first two levels: an umpire. Like zeroes, they see the limitations of their understanding and their insufficient responses. But unlike weak responders, they draw on a higher power. Instead of turning to the self for answers, these thinkers go to a higher source—a referee to call the game.

Lenses	Zero	Hero
They Say	I can't	I can
Response	Weak	Strong
Outlook	Pessimist	Optimist
Source	Self	Self
Esteem	Low	High

> Man cannot make his own universe and then live in it.
>
> Francis A. Schaeffer

CHAPTER SEVEN

Living a Lie or Having an Open Mind

I marveled when I entered the exam room. Cindy, dressed in a business suit, dipped a spoonful of green stuff into her baby's mouth. The toddler slobbered and green goop ran down her chin, almost dripping onto the mother's spotless white blouse.

In the nick of time, Cindy wiped the baby's mouth with a cloth. "Caught ya! You're too slow, Cheyenne." Cindy tickled her daughter, babbled something in baby language, and wiped another blob of slimy green stuff from her face. "Mommy's got this."

"How can I help you?" I asked, still amazed Cindy could keep green slime off her clothes.

Cindy straightened and got down to business. Pulling up her daughter's shirt, she pointed to the problem. "Cheyenne has a belly button hernia. My pediatrician sent me here for a third opinion. What do you think?"

I examined Cheyenne and easily pushed the intestines back through the small hole in the muscle. "Does it seem to bother her?"

Cindy shook her head. "No. Not a bit."

When I pushed the bulge in Cheyenne's tummy back inside the second time, the baby giggled. "What did your pediatrician tell you?"

"She said to leave it alone."

I nodded. "I think she's right. In this case, I would watch it. What did the second opinion tell you?"

Cindy pulled down Cheyenne's shirt. "I went to see another surgeon, and she told me to leave it alone."

"We don't typically operate on umbilical hernias until the age of three, and some surgeons recommend waiting until the age of five. If it's not bothering her, let's wait."

Cindy's eyes narrowed. She scrolled on her cell phone, scowled, and showed me her screen. "This site says the intestines can strangulate in an umbilical hernia and says it should be fixed before that happens."

I scanned the blog. "Yes, but this website discusses *adult* hernias—not pediatric hernias. Unlike adults, toddlers are still growing. The hole in the muscle often closes as the child grows, and the risks of fixing pediatric hernias tend to outweigh the risks of leaving them alone. If Cheyenne is not having symptoms, fixing her hernia causes more risk than watching it."

Cindy's face reddened. "So, either way, there's a risk?"

"Yes. Medicine can help us or hurt us. At times, surgery is our friend, but sometimes it can cause more damage."

She closed her eyes and exhaled. "Doctors only care about avoiding lawsuits."

Cindy released Cheyenne and watched her totter across the room. "I think I'll go for a fourth opinion. I've been burned once already by well-meaning but ill-informed doctors."

I excused myself, walked to my office, and pulled my pediatric surgery textbook off the shelf. Walking back to Cindy's room, I searched for the chapter on hernias.

There, highlighted in yellow, was the exact explanation I had given Cindy. I held my place in the book with one finger and entered Cindy's room, feeling smug and prepared for a fight.

In my absence, something had changed. Cindy cradled Cheyenne in her arms. She sniffed and wiped her eyes. "We lost our first child, Brad." Cindy put a clean towel on her shoulder and burped her baby. "I was pregnant with Cheyenne when he died. He developed a cough and fever. I went to the emergency room to have him checked out. The doctor told us the flu was going around. He ordered some Tylenol and told us Brad was okay. In thirty minutes, we were treated and discharged. No tests. No chest X-rays. Little Brad got worse that evening. He began to have trouble breathing. We took him back to the ER."

Tears fell on Cindy's jacket. I removed my finger from the book, no longer interested in proving my point.

Cheyenne fell asleep in her mom's arms. Cindy stroked her daughter's hair. "A different doctor saw Brad. He found pneumonia and a collapsed lung. They placed a tube in Brad's mouth and one in his chest."

Cindy shivered. "They put him on a breathing machine and transferred him by helicopter to a pediatric hospital. They wouldn't let me ride with him. When we got to the hospital, they told us our Brad had died on the way. The autopsy showed the doctor had placed the breathing tube in his stomach, not his lungs."

The Source of the Matter

Now I understood why Cindy was so skeptical. Anyone would have trouble trusting a physician after such a tragic experience. Cindy's skepticism rooted itself in an adverse life event. The circumstances of her first baby's death left a wound which may never heal. Interacting with physicians sprinkled salt on the wound. Cindy's painful experience made trusting anyone—especially those in the medical field—difficult and painful.

Cindy's calamity mirrors the tragedy some people experience with Christianity. Something happened. Someone experiences an event they can't get over. They've been fooled once, maybe twice. Having been burned before, they never want to experience those emotions again.

- The person who approached the pastor with sincere questions, only to receive a "just believe—don't ask questions" answer.
- The teenager who experienced a sexual assault by a youth leader.
- The student who came to church looking for encouragement, but no one noticed her. Instead of finding help, she left lonelier than when she arrived and never returned.
- The individual grieving a loved one's loss, who asks, "Why would a loving God do this to me?"
- The young family who decided to explore Christianity and found a church filled with strife, scandal, and division.

Instead of having an open mind and a healthy skepticism about the third level, some people's hearts are closed. Many cannot overcome past emotions. Instead, they choose the second level and trust only themselves.

These individuals face an emotional hurdle, not an intellectual one. Difficult experiences have impaired their ability to trust anything or anyone other than themselves. They carry an emotional grudge. Disappointed, they settle for the victim, zero, or hero mindset.

Some adopt a second-level kind of spirituality which fits their understanding of the world. They pick and choose from an array of conflicting viewpoints, content with living in the intellectual tension. Their beliefs are reinforced by culture. Disappointed by humans who claim to represent God, second-level thinkers may prefer to pick their own spirituality, one which fits their experiences.

Those with painful life experiences need to ask ourselves some tough questions.

- Like Cindy, can we trust ourselves?
- Is our finite knowledge enough to conclude that there isn't another way of seeing life?
- How should we account for the positive encounters of others?
- Are we sure our subjective experiences explain reality?

The $C + R = O$ formula doesn't answer this dilemma. If we follow this thinking to its conclusion, we may consider suicide, as Joan did. Or we could live like Wilma, second-guessing our responses, see-sawing back and forth on the second level.

Forced to Hide a Secret

Nick's dad, Norm, was a hell-fire preacher after World War II. Norm left Nick's mother at home to provide for the family while he traveled around speaking at church conferences. In Norm's absence, Nick's mom had an affair.

Norm divorced his wife, kidnapped Nick and his sister, and hid them from their mother. Norm left the children at an orphanage, then went about his business of preaching and teaching. Nick and his sister were left alone, wondering what had happened.

- Had they displeased their parents?

- Did they cause the family breakup?
- Was their abandonment their fault?

After the divorce, preacher Norm remarried. The newlyweds took Nick and his sister out of the orphanage and settled down, pastoring small churches. But there was a glitch in the blended family: no one could mention the divorce or the remarriage. Nick's father and stepmother encouraged Nick to hide their family secret.

"It was terrible," Nick said. "In our denomination, divorced pastors exclude themselves from ministry. I loved my dad and stepmom, but I had to live a lie. I was forced to call my stepmom 'mother' and had to pretend I was her biological child. Whenever we moved to a new town, our secret followed us. And when people learned about our secret, they ran us off. My dad blamed me for telling, but I never told anyone."

When Nick graduated high school, Norm pushed him to preach. Nick went to Bible school and traveled for a time with his father. However, confused by the mixed messages, Nick left and never went back.

"I couldn't live a lie anymore," he said.

Nick's reasons for abandoning his faith and his family are understandable. Nick experienced deep wounds caused by being separated from his mother, burying feelings about his family, and lying to protect his father's job.

How would we respond if placed in the same conditions?

The Issue Isn't the Issue

Obstacles to the search for a higher power aren't only emotional. Some barriers are deliberate, ones involving the will.

Paul came to shadow me. "I plan to apply for medical school after I finish college, and I need to know if this is the right career to pursue."

Paul had a scruffy beard and a keen mind.

During rounds, I noticed Paul's socks were different colors. One was orange, and one was blue.

"Are you an Auburn or Gator fan?" I asked.

"Neither." Paul's cell phone vibrated. "Sorry. That's Nicole, my fiancée."

After finishing the day, we sat and talked about careers in medicine.

"What is your major?" I asked.

"Philosophy." After quoting Kant, Kierkegaard, and Camus, Paul said, "We really can't know anything. We can only know ideas about things."

I tapped Paul's chair. "So, you believe this chair may not exist. You just think it's there?"

"Yep," he said. "It's just my perception."

"Paul, if the chair may not exist, why did you sit in it? How could you have any confidence that the chair—or whatever it is—would hold you up?"

Paul scratched his beard.

I sipped my coffee. "This sounds like a bad version of *The Matrix*. How can you function in a world where you can't distinguish between what's real and what's not?"

Paul leaned back in his chair and folded his arms behind his head. "Life is an illusion."

"You think one way, yet you live in another. It sounds like you have two realities—the one you perceive and the one which you act upon every day."

"Exactly," said Paul.

"How do you explain the reality that the chairs you sit in every day hold you up? How do you explain why you act upon the knowledge that chairs exist?" I shook my head. "Paul, I don't know if medicine is a good fit for you."

Paul leaned forward. "Why do you say that?"

"What about the lady with colon cancer? Imagine we told her, 'Well, we really don't *know* you have cancer. It may be a figment of our imagination.' What would happen?"

He laughed. "Well, that's different. That's the physical world."

"Think about it," I said. "Physicians act upon their observations—what they see and feel—and decisions must be made based upon those findings. We must live in reality. If we can't know anything, then saying we can't know anything is an absurd assumption."

The young philosopher raised his eyebrows. "You have a point."

"If you have no confidence anything is real, how can you make such a universal claim about reality? You've made assumptions which make no sense."

Before I could continue, Paul's cell phone rang. "It's Samantha, my girlfriend."

I did a double-take. "I thought Nicole was your girlfriend."

"Nope," said Paul. "Nicole is my fiancée. Samantha's on the side."

Could there be a connection between Paul's belief and his behavior? Was Paul using philosophical pondering to camouflage his behavior?

Some don't open their minds to a higher formula for a simple reason: they don't want to. They understand the implications of yielding to a higher authority. And submitting to a higher power—which makes the rules—may force a change in lifestyle. They choose to immerse themselves in a cloud of imponderable questions which they know no one can answer. If the questions can't be answered, they are free to carry on in their lifestyle.

Friedrich Nietzsche, an atheist and second-level thinker, explains this position well. "Now it is our preference which decides against Christianity, not arguments."

Instead of being intellectually honest, many people hide in a smoke-screen of questions. Most know self-autonomy is at stake.

When we take ourselves out of the center of the universe and submit to a higher power, we must adjust. Giving up the choice to determine right and wrong can be a scary proposition. Could the fear of bringing an umpire into the game be a mental crutch?

Exploring these issues takes courage, a healthy skepticism, and intellectual integrity. For many reasons, people don't explore the possibility of a higher level. Some are emotional. Others have barriers of the will. Many have a more pragmatic reason: they are too busy.

Another group exists: those with sincere questions. If given enough evidence, they would consider a different framework of thinking.

Summary of Part One

We've discussed three lower-level formulas of thought and two mental frameworks describing distinct ways of viewing life.

First, we have victim thinkers who process life events through $C = O$ lenses. Victim thinkers struggle with two hurdles. They linger on events which have already occurred and which can't be changed. They also withdraw from responsibility and fail to focus on events they can influence.

Like Tonya and Nathan, many people encounter difficult circumstances. The greatest first-level tragedy may be that victims don't have—or use—the tools to get *through* their obstacles.

The second level changes the focus from the event to the individual's response. *How we respond to what happens matters more than what happens to us* is a common theme for second-level thinkers.

Strong responders feel their attitudes and actions are enough. When they fail to measure up, there's another technique to tweak. Garth, my friend with cerebral palsy, models $C + R = O$. His solid and dynamic responses exemplify the hero formula.

Heroes possess a dark side. Champions pay a price for greatness and sometimes unintentionally hurt others. Because they can't consistently live up to the expectations of their admirers, heroes tend to hide their faults, cover up their inadequate responses, and fear being exposed.

Unlike their second-level hero colleagues, $C + r = O$ thinkers aren't as sure about their responses. Zeroes suffer from low self-esteem, insecurity, and guilt. Weak responders second-guess themselves, identifying their actions as inadequate.

Both heroes and zeroes interpret the second level through a different lens.

R = a strong, confident response
r = a weak, insecure reaction

Both types of second-level thinkers focus on the self's ability to respond to circumstances. Neither viewpoint has a framework to determine which responses are adequate. The second level adopts a relativistic worldview, relying on the individual's subjective interpretation of events, responses, and outcomes.

I suggest the hero/zero formulas fall short in another area. They do not empower individuals with the ability to consistently meet and respond to every life challenge.

SUMMARY OF PART ONE

The lower levels are not all bad. They have helpful principles we can glean from—good, true, and real things. On the victim level, there are times we need to allow others to intervene for us. Like Frank, with the embedded nail, we sometimes must defer responsibility to experts equipped to handle the situation.

Our society needs heroes with the courage to intervene in difficult circumstances. Think of the medical advances we enjoy because of surgical giants like Dr. Debakey. The advances of champions have a great impact on society and culture.

Garth's story inspires us to see our circumstances in a positive way. Many self-help insights provide valuable tools to help us understand how we can improve ourselves.

We can even learn from zeroes. Weak responders may be the most honest group of lower-level thinkers. They are somewhere in the process of coming to the end of themselves. On the third level, zeroes are in an excellent position to receive God's help.

Part Two of this book begins with the evidence for a higher power. These chapters affirm why belief in a higher power makes sense. Once the groundwork has been laid, we move into the experience of the third level.

Rather than canceling the lower levels, the third level completes them and achieves what the other formulas cannot by factoring in another element. This higher level doesn't trivialize personal responsibility or downplay our experiences. It adds a supernatural factor to the equation.

> # One who claims to be a skeptic of one set of beliefs is actually a true believer in another set of beliefs.
>
> ## Phillip E. Johnson

PART TWO

CHAPTER EIGHT

Clues to a Higher Power
Imagine three spheres or circles. Every circle supports a third level of thinking, and each one verifies itself in unique ways. Separately, the spheres provide clues to the existence of a higher power. When these circles overlap, sufficient reasons for God emerge.

The first sphere involves science, which examines the material world through the scientific method. Science weighs the validity of a hypothesis by how well it explains what we observe.

The second sphere involves something we know better than anything in the universe: ourselves. This realm explores human intuition, consciousness, and moral feelings. Philosophers call this circle Ontology. Others call it human nature.

The third sphere involves history. This circle of knowledge verifies events and people in many ways. Historians ask, "Did the event in question really happen? Was it fact, fiction, or fantasy?"

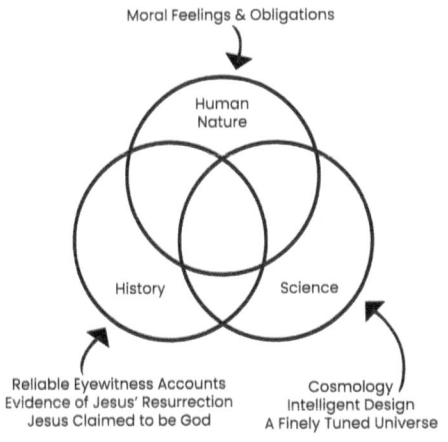

A Diagnosis Looking for a Patient

Joanna, a twenty-year-old, developed fever, nausea, and a mild headache. She visited a neurologist who concluded three possibilities: an aneurysm, a brain tumor, or meningitis. At her visit, Joanna developed diarrhea and a stomachache.

"It could still be meningitis," said the neurologist. In haste, the doctor sent her through a series of expensive tests, all of which were normal.

The neurologist performed a lumbar puncture. He stuck a needle in her back, testing the fluid around her brain. All the while, Joanna's bowel issues progressed. She fainted after the procedure and had to be admitted to the hospital.

"She might have pellagra," said the neurologist. "It's characterized by the three *d*'s: diarrhea, dementia, and death."

More esoteric tests were ordered, and specialists were consulted. The gastroenterologist suggested it could be Crohn's disease.

After a colonoscopy excluded Crohn's disease, a surgical consultation was obtained. "It could be appendicitis," said the surgeon.

Before Joanna's appendix was removed, she improved—despite her doctors. She had caught a stomach bug: common, simple, and easy to explain. In retrospect, she may have been better off at home, without multiple specialists and expensive, harmful tests.

I was engaged to Joanna during this time. Watching my fiancée suffer, this physician-in-training learned some lessons.

- First, exclude the most probable possibilities. Common things are common.
- If those explanations don't work, consider the rare, more uncommon ailments.
- If symptoms don't fit, *don't make them fit*. An open mind considers every possibility.

Instead of starting with Joanna's symptoms, making observations, and fitting them into a diagnosis, my future wife's doctors placed their favorite maladies on her and tried to make them fit. Joanna's doctors began with hunches and followed each assumption down its path. They failed to stop and consider whether they were on the right track.

We tend to make assumptions about people, only to realize our first impressions were wrong. We experience something and conclude every subsequent similar event will be the same. And when the scenario changes, we must backtrack and rethink things.

I can't be too hard on Joanna's doctors. I have done the same. I have operated on patients based on an incorrect hunch—and sometimes, my hunches have caused more harm than good.

Like Joanna's doctors, many scientists give esoteric, uncommon explanations without evaluating their framework of thinking. They assume God doesn't exist, presuppose the material world is the only reality, and exclude data suggesting otherwise.

Many people *believe* that belief in God is unscientific and closed-minded. Thus, they throw out any possibility of a third level. They argue that no evidence exists for God and base their claims on science.

Are these assumptions true? Are God and science mutually exclusive?

How we answer these questions depends upon our level of thinking.

Volumes of books discuss the scientific rationale for a higher power. Here, we'll discuss only enough information to introduce these topics and explain why reasonable people place God into their framework.

First, let's consider cosmology. Most scientists agree the universe began at a specific place and time. Findings of the twentieth century suggest the universe is expanding.

- In the 1930s, Hubble noticed galaxies were moving away from each other.
- Hubble's findings correlate with the Second Law of Thermodynamics and fit into Einstein's theories of relativity.
- The presence of radiation afterglow suggests the universe began at a point in time.

Like a hot cup of coffee puts off heat as it cools, our universe emits radiation. The presence—or mere existence—of this radiation suggests a young universe, one which is not as old as many suppose. In an eternal or old universe, the "coffee" would already be cold. There would be no radiation. Residual radiation can be best explained by a cosmos with a beginning.

With an expanding cosmos, scientists can rewind the celestial clock. Physicists no longer have grounds to suggest an eternal universe. To keep God out of the equation, naturalists must maintain that something came from nothing.

Non-theists are left scratching their heads, having no rational explanation of origins. The very science atheists use to explain a universe without a creator speaks against them. Atheist and astrophysicist, Robert Jastrow, explains the dilemma well.

> For the scientist who has lived by his faith in the power of reason, the story ends like a bad dream. He has scaled the mountain of ignorance; he is about to conquer the highest peak; as he pulls himself over the final rock, he is greeted by a band of theologians who have been sitting there for centuries.

Theists have a simple explanation for a beginning. Something came from *something*. Moving on from cosmology, theists maintain the universe is tailored for life as we know it.

- Physical constants, like gravity, are perfectly tuned for life to exist.
- The sun's size, age, and location create a safe place for life in the cosmos.
- The earth's position from the sun is like the porridge in the story of Goldilocks: not too hot or too cold.
- The earth's size, circular orbit, rotational speed, and axis provide conditions fit for life.
- The unique composition of the earth's elements provides a perfect mix of all needed ingredients.

If one of the above factors changes by any degree, the possibility of life as we understand it becomes impossible. The fabric of the universe seems to be tweaked—are these factors mere coincidence?

Anthropic studies, which apply probabilities to the existence of human life, show more than one hundred of these "coincidences." Author

Stephen Meyer calculated these factors and found that the possibility of life as we know it occurring by chance is about 1 in 10^{138}.

Let's put these overwhelming numbers in perspective. The total number of atoms in the observable cosmos is around 10^{78}—a rough estimate of ten quadrillion vigintillion. In other words, if you could mark one atom, throw it into the expanse of the universe, and then search for it, your chance of finding that specific atom is one in 10^{78}.

Good luck on your quest.

The number of atoms in the cosmos pales in comparison with 10^{138}. The probability of putting all the coincidences together to produce life as we know it approaches the inconceivable. How much faith does it take to bet on such an improbability?

Like Joanna's doctor, many bet on uncommonly uncommon possibilities—even when the odds are stacked against them. They speculate on the long shot, even with a 1 in 10^{138} chance of winning the bet.

Intelligent Design

Two hundred years ago, William Paley proposed teleological arguments. If someone stumbles upon a watch, examines its details carefully, and considers the possibilities, a reasonable person will conclude the watch was made by an intelligent being—a watchmaker.

Fifty years later, Darwin proposed the opposite idea: the *appearance* of design without a designer. Darwin's theories didn't attempt to describe how life originated. He explained how species which already existed changed over time. His proposition was easier to make in the 1850s, when the complexity of genetic information was unknown.

Many started down this intellectual path and believed Darwin's presuppositions. Although new findings have placed roadblocks in this framework of thinking, many plod forward rather than reevaluate their assumptions.

Through science, we now grasp the intricacy of systems found in cells. And new technology makes explaining origins from naturalistic theories problematic. Evolution, for example, has no reasonable explanation for how DNA (deoxyribonucleic acid) came into being.

The self-assembly model, which assumes DNA aggregates on its own, has some big problems. If nucleotides could come together spontaneously through a random process, the genetic message would be garbled. DNA would behave more like crystals and lose the capability to create the diversity seen in cell proteins. Crystals carry minimal information. In self-assembly theories, DNA loses specificity. The message becomes redundant, which makes protein differentiation impossible.

Others suggest DNA came through retrograde mechanisms—a reverse process in which proteins came first. This proposal faces another roadblock: how did proteins originate?

The banner study, which naturalists propose answered the question, was performed in the 1950s. Stanley Miller created a primordial soup and then zapped it with an electric current, which simulated a pre-life environment. Under these conditions, small amino acids spontaneously generated.

Evolutionists declared the protein dilemma solved. Proteins generated in the primordial goo could be translated into DNA through a reverse process, and science could finally explain how DNA originated.

As a first-year biology major, I listened to my professor explain how Miller's research confirmed naturalism.

"Evolution is a fact, and these studies prove it. If proteins can be generated, then proteins could give rise to DNA. Life is not only possible through natural processes but is also highly probable."

These "facts" perplexed me, and I wondered which authority to believe—my professor or my preacher. Years later, I learned my professor had not divulged the deficiencies in the research.

Skeptics suggest Miller rigged the experiment. The composition of Miller's soup differed from the makeup believed to exist in pre-life conditions. And Miller's proteins were siphoned out of the broth, protecting them from the current which created them. If those peptides had remained in the soup, the same electricity which generated them would have caused their demise.

Dr. Miller's scientific methods had flaws. Skeptics argue the designer of the experiment created suitable conditions. Were Miller's design details and my professor's presentation of the results simple oversights, or were these claims rooted in intellectual bias—a mental framework predisposed to disbelieving in a watchmaker?

Probability poses a problem for protein theories. According to Stephen Meyer, author of *Signature in the Cell*, the occurrence of self-assembling proteins is inconceivably small.

"I show that the probability of producing even a single functional protein of modest length (150 amino acids) by chance alone in a prebiotic environment stands at no better than a 'vanishingly small' 1 chance in 10^{164}."

Irreducible Complexity and Devolution

The issue with believing in design without a designer goes beyond genetics. Cell biologists who investigate the validity of naturalistic theories ask, "Does evolution fit what is observed on a cellular level?"

Michael Behe, a biochemist, argues that cellular structures are too complicated to develop haphazardly. Evolution proposes small changes occur over long periods. Given time, chance, and the right conditions, naturalist theories maintain complex cellular systems *could* develop.

The problem with naturalism lies in the complexity of cellular structures. Many cell systems are irreducibly complex. For these traits to be propagated into subsequent generations, every piece of the system must be functional—any item without a current function will be thrown out.

Biologists argue these systems could not have evolved bit by bit. Each part couldn't have evolved separately over long periods. Harsh selective processes would have discarded them long before they were used.

All structural parts must exist—simultaneously—for the whole system to function. And there lies the rub. Evolution has no reasonable explanation for how irreducibly complex systems developed.

Behe also maintains that observed mutations contradict natural selection theories. Evolution suggests that species *gain* function through mutation. Observational evidence implies the opposite. Behe suggests that species change by the *loss* of genetic function.

This occurs for one simple reason. In nature, loss of function is *easier* than a gain of function. While functional gains require multiple complex changes to occur in sequence, functional losses require one glitch. The simple concept suggests it is easier to tear down something than to build it by chance. Behe's works provide multiple examples of what he calls "devolution."

With new findings in biochemistry, cell biology, and genetics, the possibility of an intelligent higher power becomes understandable.

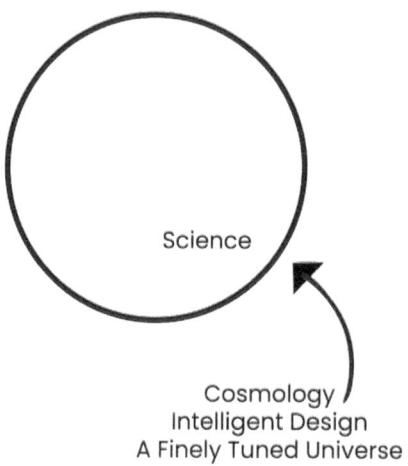

Francis Bacon, a third-level thinker and scientist, summed up the scientific sphere.

"A little science estranges a man from God. A lot of science brings him back."

I have introduced four major topics within the circle of science.

- Cosmology: current scientific findings point toward a beginning.
- Anthropic principle: the finely tuned universe has been fitted for life as we know it.
- Intelligent Design: systems—like DNA and cell structures—are irreducibly complex.
- Devolution: mutational observations counter the assumption that life is evolving and show a tendency for a loss rather than a gain of function.

Many thinkers see a reasonable, straightforward explanation for thesecontroversies. Complex molecular systems, DNA, and the cosmos were made by a designer. They agree with Paley. An intricate watch—the world we live in—can best be explained by the presence of a watchmaker.

In this whirlwind of information, here are three take-home points:

- Third-level experts who believe in a higher power haven't committed intellectual suicide.
- Many third-level thinkers provide solid, verifiable reasons for their mental framework.
- Both sides in the controversy express faith in a set of intellectual assumptions.

Science alone doesn't get us there. Jumping to a third level of thinking based on this one circle isn't enough. We need to explore another sphere outside things we can place in a test tube.

Many believe knowledge can only be verified through empirical data—what can be observed and tested through science. If this assertion is valid, how do we explain mathematics and logic?

These two disciplines, which can't be proved scientifically, are the bedrock of science. Without mathematics, scientists cannot measure or study things. Without logic, observers cannot distinguish between one observation and another. Scientists must presuppose the validity of math and reason to perform experiments and interpret data.

These intellectual assumptions come from another circle of knowledge: human intuition. Although we can't prove math and logic empirically, we know they are true. Intuition helps us grasp the necessity of a third level and a higher power.

Consciousness and Moral Obligation

Katrin pulled onto the freeway. A stalled car on the roadside obstructed the flow of traffic. Katrin edged closer and turned up her windshield wipers. The car had a flat tire. A lone, frail woman tried to lift a heavy jack.

If Katrin pulled over to help, she'd have to return home to change her wet clothes, and she was already late. She might lose her job. But that woman couldn't change the tire alone. Katrin flicked her blinker and eased onto the shoulder. Just ahead of her, two other drivers moved over to help.

What made Katrin want to help, and why did others have the same notion? Where did the idea originate that someone should act?

Katrin felt a moral obligation to stop. This urge can't be explained by sociobiology. Katrin's altruistic feelings for someone she didn't know wouldn't get her genes into the next generation. In fact, fixing the flat tire might expose her to harm. She could lose her job—or maybe her life—for doing a good deed.

These feelings go beyond instinct and are practiced in every culture. Every day, people do kind things: deeds which can't be explained with naturalistic theories and courageous acts without regard to self-interest or self-protection.

These moral urges should tell us something. Why do we want to help people we don't know when there is no biological benefit? Do these moral feelings remind us of an external reference, something which exists beyond ourselves? Could we be more than cosmic accidents?

In chapter five, we discussed the urge to respect, admire, and honor others. Moral expectations we place on others are coupled with the desire to put those individuals on a pedestal. We believe our heroes should respond in specific ways. When they act as champions, we worship them.

Humans possess strong moral feelings, obligations we believe should be met. Could these expectations give clues to a higher power?

Would it not be strange if a universe without purpose accidentally created humans who are so obsessed with purpose?

Sir John Templeton

CHAPTER NINE

The Puzzle Pieces and the Puzzle Box

So far, we've touched on science and one aspect of human nature: the things we *ought* to do. When other people violate a moral code or when we see occurrences we feel shouldn't happen, we cry for justice.

In northern Pakistan, a small hospital serves a poor, isolated region. It lies north of Abbottabad, the town where Bin Laden hid away. In the early 1990s, I traveled to the hospital as a medical student.

One evening, a young family came to the hospital. The wife was in labor but failing to progress. The baby's head was too large to pass through the birth canal. The ultrasound confirmed the baby was a girl.

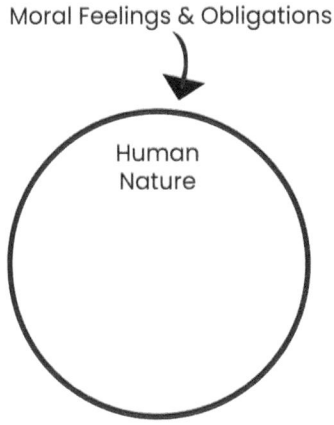

Dr. Luke talked with the husband and recommended a C-section. The husband responded in Urdu, "Koee baat nahin."

"What did he say?" I asked.

Dr. Luke scratched his head. "He said, 'It doesn't matter.'"

I did a double-take. "He's going to let his wife and the baby die?"

After a long, heated discussion with the husband, Dr. Luke took me aside. "The husband says his wife isn't worth the twelve hundred rupees it will cost to have the C-section. If the baby had been a boy, he would have paid for it."

"Is he out of his mind? Heck, I'll pay the twelve hundred rupees for the surgery. It's only about fifty bucks."

Dr. Luke sighed. "We offered him the surgery for free. He doesn't want to proceed. Some people here see women as property, no different from cows and goats. Women have more value if they bring boys into the family."

Later, the husband decided to proceed with surgery. Tragically, the window of opportunity had closed. The mother and her baby died.

Whether in Pakistan or Pennsylvania, something wells up within us when individuals make unjust decisions. Something inside transcends cultures, geography, religious beliefs, gender, and skin color to tell us the husband's actions were wrong.

Where do these strong moral feelings originate?

When we listen to people, we find they have strong beliefs, and they believe these moral feelings apply to everyone.

Our awareness of moral obligations—what people should and shouldn't do—can be best explained by a reference external to man. With few exceptions, humans agree upon these assumptions. These universal understandings exist outside of the self.

When people—individuals, families, businesses, or nations—argue, they assume the opposing party believes in both a moral conscience and in moral truths: realities which hold everyone accountable.

Arguments are based on the opposing side's violation of an absolute. Both sides, perhaps subconsciously, agree upon this external reference. Parties quarrel using this external reference, seldom recognizing its existence.

Without an objective standard beyond man, we're left with second-level relativism. And if moral feelings are arbitrary, man has no basis for imposing any obligation on another.

The presence of moral urges should lead us to consider a reference point beyond ourselves. These standards help us understand why a third level of thinking makes sense. This clue, unlike science, cannot be measured through empirical methods.

Intuitively, individuals refer to codes outside of themselves—values to which they hold all people.

The Christian worldview explains how these moral feelings exist and where they originate. These urges do not originate from man, the players in the game. These thoughts of consciousness remind us of an umpire, an external reference point, a higher power.

Third-level thinkers take the next step, declaring moral laws are defined in the Bible. Christians believe these moral urges can be authenticated through history. Like no other reference, the Bible roots itself in history, which allows its claims to be verified.

The Third Sphere: History
To determine a book's credibility, historians evaluate texts from different viewpoints. Scholars call the process of examining the Bible *textual criticism*.

Reliable Eyewitness Accounts
Evidence of Jesus' Resurrection
Jesus Claimed to be God

Discussions of all the historical facts and propositions isn't possible in one book. We will focus on two specific concepts on which everything hinges: Jesus's assertions that he was God and the claims of a resurrection. If these are true, valid reasons exist to become a third-level thinker.

Two hikers, Brad and Beth, stumble upon a clearing in the woods. A violin rests against a tree stump ahead of them. Brad picks up the instrument, wipes rosin off the wood, and plucks the metal strings. "Wow, this fiddle is in tune. Someone must have left it by the tree."

Beth looks around. "I don't see footprints or signs of anyone." She takes the violin from Brad and runs her fingers over the strings. "Well, the fact that it's in tune is simply coincidence."

Brad examines it thoroughly. "This appears to be handmade. See the initials carved on the inside? Look. The fingerboard is worn. See how the oil from the player's hand has changed the surface where his fingers have played? This violin must have incredible value."

Beth laughs. "You've got to be kidding. Nobody wants that old, worn-out relic. If it's so valuable, why did they leave it here? It's ours now. Finders keepers."

Brad sits on the stump and sighs. "Beth, this fiddle is not ours to take. I'll bet the owner will come back and get it."

Beth shakes her head. "Brad, you have no real evidence—only conjecture. We've caught our breath. Let's move on."

Brad leans the violin back on the stump. "You're not looking at the big picture. You can't explain why it's here."

Beth turns to head up the trail. "I don't need an explanation. All I can say is, it's here."

Brad and Beth continue down the trail, arguing about the violin and arguing about the existence of a violin owner.

Eavesdropping on the conversation, we learn some things about Beth and Brad.

- Brad believes in an owner. Beth believes in coincidence.
- Both travelers present facts, have faith, and express their feelings.
- Both believers possess a mental framework to process data.

What would happen if the violin owner returned during their discussion and played his fiddle? Brad and Beth would have proof of a fiddler. The discussion would be over.

The historical sphere completes the framework of why a third level makes sense. Christians believe the fiddler came and gave an unforgettable performance, and this event was verified before eyewitnesses.

RELIABLE EYEWITNESS ACCOUNTS

Unlike science, historical events happen only once and can't be repeated. If we weren't present when the fiddler returned, we would have to take Brad and Beth's word on the subject.

History determines what happened based on the testimony of eyewitnesses—individuals who experienced the event.

Christianity hinges on the events involving the life of Jesus. In contrast to other belief systems, the accounts of Jesus's life circumstances and how he responded to them can be examined and substantiated.

Several of Jesus's followers wrote down his story. They experienced the events of Jesus's life and death firsthand. Although each recorded the events in their unique way, they all shared the same message.

- Jesus claimed to be God.
- Jesus demonstrated his claims by performing miracles.
- Jesus suffered false accusations and died at the hands of his persecutors.
- Jesus rose from the dead, verifying his claim to be God.

Reliable Eyewitness Accounts
The Bible, on one level, can be evaluated as a historical document. The accounts of Jesus's life events occurred in a specific place and time.

- Jesus was born in Palestine, in the first century A.D., the time of Augustus and Herod the Great, in an era called the Pax Romana.
- While still in the womb, Jesus was enrolled in a Roman census.
- His death and resurrection occurred during a Jewish Passover feast.
- Pontius Pilate, his judge, ruled in Palestine from 26-36 A.D.

The events regarding Jesus are rooted in history.

If these stories were myths, we would expect exaggerations—especially from the disciples. Jesus's followers, who recorded the events, were honest about themselves. They didn't present themselves as heroes in the story.

Instead of embellishing things, they documented their faults and misunderstandings about Jesus and his teachings. The disciples even shared their disbelief, especially when examining the resurrection event. Thomas, for example, doubted Jesus's bodily resurrection. He asked for evidence and wanted to palpate Jesus's wounds. These documented accounts are realistic and honest—something we would not expect if the story were a fantasy.

If the disciples were lying, perhaps involved in a cover-up scheme, no one would expect them to stick to their story. Instead of receiving fame or money, the eyewitnesses were persecuted. Most were killed for sharing their observations. Despite the pressure to recant their experiences, none changed the confession.

Unlike other great teachers who taught about God, Jesus claimed to be more than a great thinker, leader, or educator. Jesus declared himself to be God. The validity of this claim lies in the resurrection. If Jesus rose from the dead, we can conclude the claims are true.

Can these allegations be authenticated?

Several theories explain what could have happened. The swoon hypothesis claims Jesus never died. After his asphyxiation, the executioners punctured his chest with a spear. Convinced Jesus was dead, they took him off the cross, but the soldiers didn't break his legs. Their assessment was straightforward: dead people don't limp away. The trained executioners left well enough alone. Experienced soldiers were convinced of Jesus's death.

Others suggest Jesus died, but thieves stole his body and faked the resurrection. If the disciples stole the body, how did they do it? How did they overcome well-trained soldiers commanded to keep watch? The soldiers, charged to guard the grave, placed their lives and honor at risk. No group could overpower these fighting men. The assumption anyone stole his body is improbable.

Perhaps Jewish leaders paid off the soldiers and hid Jesus's body, fearing others would steal it. If this occurred, the leaders would have produced the body as evidence to squelch the post-resurrection crowds who claimed Jesus had risen. The Rabbis had no answer for an empty tomb.

The transformation of the disciples after the resurrection is another puzzle. The pre- and post-resurrection responses of Jesus's followers were very different. Before, they operated as victims, heroes, or zeroes. Afterward, they seemed to function on a higher level.

RELIABLE EYEWITNESS ACCOUNTS

Before the resurrection, they were fearful of the synagogue leaders and of public opinion, but something changed after the resurrection. All the eyewitnesses stuck to the story, despite persecution. They didn't try to save their skins—even under the pressure of death.

The narrative of Jesus's postmortem appearances has a unique flavor: women saw him first. If the resurrection stories were embellished, no one would expect women to be the first to encounter Jesus's resurrected body. At first, the disciples didn't believe the women's reports. In first-century culture, women had the least credibility, so an author trying to write a believable story at that time would not place a woman in an important role.

The writers presented realistic accounts of what occurred at the tomb and what subsequently happened. They gave honest representations of themselves. If these accounts were legends, one would not expect the writers to portray themselves as fickle, undecided, and unsure about what they had seen.

Thomas, in particular, approached the event with intellectual honesty and skepticism. He saw Jesus resurrected. Thomas confirmed what had been said and believed the evidence.

When considering the historical sphere, one main question needs to be verified.

Was Jesus truly God, and did he rise from the dead?

These testimonials can be examined and verified. In those accounts, Jesus claims to be more than a teacher showing us the way. Jesus claimed to *be* the way. Supporting this assertion, writers went into great detail about Jesus's death and resurrection.

The Bible doesn't expect skeptics to believe without asking questions. It does quite the opposite. The Bible encourages honest people like Thomas to examine the evidence, ask questions, and come to their own conclusions.

Those who don't believe in a higher power *can't* assume several things:

- Anyone who adds another element to their mental equation is ignorant and closed-minded.
- Faith excludes reason. Many intellectually honest people base their beliefs on verifiable evidence.

- Reason excludes faith. Everyone's mental framework believes something.

This doesn't present an airtight rationale for a higher power. We've explored three categories giving credibility to God's existence. These three circles employ unique proofs of a higher reality. Evaluating these spheres should provoke some questions.

- How credible are the things in which we believe?
- Which possibility gives us the most reasonable explanation for the evidence?
- Which belief has the greatest probability of fitting what we experience in reality?

Christianity doesn't suggest believing something makes it true. Christianity asserts that something's credibility makes it believable.

Sufficient reasons exist to believe in the God of the Bible. Experiencing the third level requires acting upon this knowledge and begins with a shift in thinking.

*T*he Christian worldview is more consistent, more rational, and more workable than any other belief system. It beats out all other contenders in giving credible answers to the great questions that any worldview must answer: Where did we come from? (creation); What is the human dilemma? (fall); and What can we do to solve the dilemma? (redemption). And the way we see the world guides the way we work to change the world (restoration).

Charles Colson

CHAPTER TEN

Galileo, a Blind Man, and a Personal Secret

Gil developed a sharp ache in his belly. Over several hours, the pain intensified. Any kind of movement worsened the symptoms. Eventually, the pain rested over the appendix.

In the emergency room, the surgeon pushed on Gil's abdomen. "You have appendicitis and need an operation."

Gil had never undergone surgery. Facing a crossroads, he had lots of questions and little assurance. Gil had several options.

- He could ask for more studies to confirm the diagnosis.
- He could search the internet for alternative options.
- He could question the surgeon's credibility and ask for a second opinion.
- He could exit the hospital and leave things up to fate.
- He could wait to see what happened.

Gil had to make an informed choice. He needed to assure himself of the evidence before proceeding. The next decision rested upon his confidence in the surgeon. Would the surgeon botch the operation? And what would he experience?

Like Gil, many people wrestle with placing their future into the hands of someone other than themselves. This degree of trust goes beyond evidence. Stepping into this way of thinking requires a mental shift.

A Geocentric Universe

For generations, people believed the earth was the center of the universe. Over time, astronomers noticed things which didn't fit into their framework. One observation involved retrograde motion. The planets moved one way across the night sky. Then, for no apparent reason, they backtracked in the other direction.

No one could explain the oddity until Copernicus. The astronomer challenged the earth-centered model. Copernicus proposed a sun-centered universe in which the earth and planets revolved around the sun: a heliocentric worldview.

Later, Galileo verified this theory with a new form of technology, the telescope. Galileo turned his scope to the heavens, and with a magnified view, he found evidence for a heliocentric universe.

Ultimately, Copernicus and Galileo's model won the day. What made the world shift its thinking? Evidence. The observable facts fit better into a heliocentric worldview.

A Shift in Perspective

In the last chapter, we considered credible reasons to believe in God. These reasons provide a framework for intellectually honest people. When these three circles of knowledge are superimposed, we have a justification for adding another element into our thinking.

Acting upon this evidence will produce a shift in thinking. This paradigm shift resembles the move from a geocentric to a heliocentric universe. The mental shift displaces the self from the center and puts God in its place. Like the change to a sun-centered model, placing God in the center of the universe involves a paradigm shift.

THE QUALITIES OF A NEW ELEMENT

This reversal can be an unsettling proposition. Moving to a God-centered mindset has some unsettling implications:

- Surrendering a self-centered focus.
- Releasing control of life's circumstances.
- Realizing the inadequacy of weak self-responses.
- Seeing life's outcome through a different set of lenses.
- Becoming accountable to a power greater than self.

The Qualities of a New Element
Three unique attributes distinguish the new element added on the third level:

- The introduction of moral absolutes.
- The possibility of relating to a *personal* God, one desiring to be known.
- A way of living where approval isn't based upon performance.

Absolutes vs. Arbitrary Absolutes
A God-centered equation embraces universals. Most people never think about the need for universals until they are wronged.

Bill goes to the bank with his paycheck and deposits $1,000. The teller returns a receipt, which says $100. When Bill sees the discrepancy, he says, "Sir, you're missing a zero. You have omitted a decimal place on my deposit."

The teller responds, "Well, I believe your deposit is only one hundred dollars."

None of us, including Bill, would accept a deposit of one-tenth the value. Absolutes become very important in this circumstance. Bill would quickly show the teller the evidence—his check stub.

Equations remind us of absolutes—principles which do not change based upon circumstances. An absolute helps us measure responses against a standard. An equation without absolutes doesn't make sense. $2 + 2 = 4$. Algebraic expressions leave no wiggle room. Math grounds itself in universals.

Every third grader understands this principle. When a student gives an incorrect answer, like $3 \times 3 = 10$, the teacher counts it wrong. The teacher doesn't say, "It's okay, Herb. The answer can be ten if you want it to be."

This construct opposes modern thinking, which says $2 + 2 = 5$ can be true depending upon the circumstances.

A Personal God
Christianity distinguishes itself from other worldviews based on a personal relationship—a trait other ways of thinking have trouble explaining.

Naturalism proclaims personal beings arose from impersonal forces. With time and chance, natural selection produced beings with the ability to:

- express emotions,
- possess an aptitude for thinking,
- express unique personality traits,
- model altruistic behavior, and
- have feelings of purpose.

How did these attributes occur based on natural selection?

From introspective thinkers to friendly, extroverted, expressive individuals, evolution cannot provide reasonable explanations of how personality develops. How can an evolutionist explain a mother's love toward her disabled child?

Most Eastern religions have the same tension as naturalists do. Why would a distant, impersonal deity produce beings who desire to know and be known relationally?

Christianity doesn't have this problem. It begins with a relatable, personal God. The Someone—God in three Persons—existed before the cosmos ever came into being.

The Christian faith says this personal God can be known. It declares that God initiated the possibility of being known through a relationship. The historical Jesus wrapped himself in human flesh so humanity could relate to God.

Performance and Acceptance
In contrast to a performance mindset, consumed by the need to *do* something, the third level begins with acceptance based on what God has already *done*.

God's acceptance, according to other religions, flows from performance. God's approval—or disapproval—depends on how people respond to their circumstances.

- Allah requires rituals.
- Hinduism promises rewards in the next life for today's deeds.
- Judaism involves keeping the law.
- Buddhism proposes the eight-fold path to Nirvana.
- New Age thought expects followers to improve responses with self-help techniques.

From an equation standpoint, these belief systems are fundamentally the same. Each is a derivative of the $C + R = O$ level of thinking and is focused on approval rooted in performance. On the second level, divine acceptance depends on how well we respond. Better responses result in higher approval.

In a sense, these worldviews focus on measuring up through self-effort, but each of these second-level beliefs is vague in defining how much is enough. They fail to specify how many good deeds are needed to cross into the realm of God's acceptance.

In some form or fashion, other worldviews suggest, "I perform. Therefore, I am accepted." The Christian faith says the reverse: "I am accepted. Therefore, I perform."

The lower levels are motivated by obligation. These worldviews live in fear of not meeting the standard. God's love motivates Christ-followers to perform out of appreciation and gratitude. They have received undeserved approval based on God's response to their circumstances.

Level	Means of Approval	Motivation
$C + R = O$	Self-effort	Fear and Obligation
$G(C+R) = O$	God-effort	Love and Gratitude

The focus changes from what we must do to meet the standard to what God has done to help us. Christianity views performance through a different grid, declaring God's approval is based not in what we do but in whom we believe.

Christianity declares that self-responses never meet God's standards. No matter how well we perform, our responses are inadequate in God's eyes. Left to ourselves, we're all zeroes—or perhaps we're victims needing a hero to intervene.

God took the initiative. Jesus took the first step, entering space and time, doing for humankind what we couldn't do.

The G Factor

The missing factor in the equation is grace. This element explains a relatable God who accepts us based upon *His* performance. The *G* factor represents God's work of grace in and through our life's situations.

G represents God's gift of favor or God's generosity.

The *G* factor expresses God's unearned and undeserved help in our circumstances. Third-level responses draw upon this factor to meet life's challenges. Third-level thinkers add the *G* factor to their mental framework. Grace changes the whole equation.

$$G(C + R) = O$$

The *G* factor empowers responses which move us toward a purposeful end: a transformed outcome. Grace thinkers see circumstances through a different set of lenses.

Vince came to my office after missing his three-year follow-up. I was prepared for a routine visit, but something about Vince had changed. He didn't look up when I entered the room.

"Howdy, Vince. You're long overdue for a scope. I'm glad you're back."

Instead of looking at me, Vince turned away and stared at the wall. "Dr. Chuck, are you sure I need another colonoscopy?"

"Yep," I replied. "You missed your follow-up. It's better to have those polyps lassoed before they turn into cancer."

Vince seemed to aim his ear toward me as I spoke.

"You had some huge polyps, and you need to be followed closely. If you don't, you may get colon cancer." I waved my hand in front of his face. Vince didn't blink his eyes or react to my hand gestures. "Vince, is something wrong?"

He nodded. "I can only see from the corner of one eye. To see you, I have to look at the wall."

Vince's odd behavior began to make sense.

Vince folded his hands. "A lot has happened since I last saw you. About the time of my last procedure, I began losing my sight. Two years ago, my wife died."

Tears clouded Vince's eyes. "I'm legally blind." Without wiping away his tears, Vince continued. "This is a journey I didn't want and never expected. But I'm thankful. I needed it. God blessed me with blindness. Now I see life in a way I could never see before."

Vince's loss of physical sight enhanced his spiritual vision. His blindness helped him look through a new set of lenses to see resources he never knew were available.

Vince's loss of vision changed his focal point. Grace helped him understand his circumstances in a new way. His faith response enhanced his spiritual ability to see a reality previously unknown. He now viewed his life challenges through the lenses of grace.

Lenses	Victim	Hero/Zero	Grace
Equation	$C = O$	$C + R = O$	$G(C + R) = O$
Focus	Life events	Self-Responses	God's help
Level	First	Second	Third

The Life Equation

$G(C + R) = O$ introduces a new mental framework.

- A mindset based upon a set of universals.
- The possibility of relating to a God who desires to be known.
- A lifestyle in which performance flows from acceptance.

The Power of the G Factor

Factors differ from terms. Factors express greater power.

Consider the equation: $3 + 4 = Y$. When the two terms, 3 and 4, are added together, the outcome, Y, depends solely on addition. Factors function by the power of multiplication. Let's add X to our equation to grasp a factor's influence.

$$X(3 + 4) = Y$$

If X equals 2, the equation looks like this:

$$2(3 + 4) = 14$$

What if X were 100? X could be 1000.
If so, do the math:

$$1000(3 + 4) = 7000$$

In the same way, the *G* factor transforms the formula through multiplication. It possesses tremendous potential to change the outcome by working through our responses and circumstances. In a sense, grace's impact can be large or small, depending upon our faith response.

MY "COME TO JESUS" MEETING

Third-level thinkers never underestimate the work of God's kindness. The influence and impact of God's generosity go beyond what the mind can imagine.

$$G = \infty$$

I feel compelled to get this off my chest: I'm allergic to math. I wasn't the kid who aced the algebra test and broke the curve. No one asked me to help with homework, and none of my classmates ever asked, "Hey, Chuck, what answer did you get on number twelve?"

If I'm terrible at mathematics, why am I writing a book using mathematical expressions?

That's how the G factor works. God often takes the most unlikely people and plants ideas in their brains. And then, grace won't let them go until they complete the task. The G factor introduced another strange notion into my head: medicine.

My parents owned a tree farm and neither went to college. I didn't have a desire to pursue medicine at a young age. I wanted to play guitar in a rock band.

Late in high school, grace took hold of me and began to carry me places. I developed a strange compulsion to pursue medicine. One day, everything caught up to me. My mathematically challenged brain and my medically unsophisticated background were put to the test.

This incident happened during my first semester of college. And, of course, it occurred in my pre-Calculus class. I failed my first math exam and needed to drop the class. Not only did I bomb algebra, but I also squeaked by my other pre-med exams—a foreboding sign.

My "Come to Jesus" Meeting

My college had a reputation for getting kids into medical school. They claimed every student who applied got accepted. The college recruiters failed to disclose a vital piece of information. They didn't explain *how* they were so successful.

After failing my math test, I went to my college advisor, slumped in my chair, and buried my face in my hands. "Sir, I made a fifty on my precalculus exam. If I fail math, I'll mess up my GPA and never get into med school."

Poker-faced, my mentor said, "Chuck, your SAT scores are below average, and your high school grades are terrible. I think it's time we have a 'come to Jesus' meeting."

"What do you mean?" I asked.

"Our pre-med curriculum culls the students who don't have what it takes early in the process. Quit now and cut your losses."

My advisor's discouraging words made my head spin. I left his office doubting whether I should continue. I felt like I had been run over by an eighteen-wheeler and almost gave up on my dream.

After a time of reflection and prayer, I decided to finish out the semester. I dropped the math class and finished my pre-med classes. I can neither explain nor take credit for my success that semester. Or the next. Or the next. What happened defies explanation.

God's generosity equipped and empowered me to finish the semester with a 4.0 grade point average.

$$G(C + R) = O$$

From a second-level perspective, things didn't add up. Another factor had been added to the equation.

- God's generosity had a purpose, an outcome for my life.
- God's kindness implanted desires and passions in my mind.
- The *G* factor enhanced my responses.
- Grace brought me through difficult circumstances.

A paradigm shift occurred, one where God became the hero of the story.

Lens	Motivation	Attitude	Acceptance
Hero/Zero	Fear and obligation	Being the best	Performance-based approval
Grace	Love and gratitude	Doing your best	Approval-based performance

Mathematics is the language with which God has written the universe.

Galileo Galilei

CHAPTER ELEVEN

An African Artist and a Truck Driver

Malawi, nicknamed "the warm heart of Africa," is one of the least developed places in the world. Many regions in this sub-Saharan country have no electricity, paved roads, or clean water. People sleep in thatched huts, cook over open fires, and farm with stone-age tools.

Many Malawians receive God's generous gift of grace. Hearing how God has done something for them they couldn't do on their own is good news.

I met Chrisford in Malawi's capital, Lilongwe. He sells hand-printed pictures to tourists—prints of women carrying buckets of water on their heads, drawings of men fishing on Lake Malawi. What's unique about Chrisford's sketches isn't their quality. What stands out is the way he creates them: he uses his teeth to create art.

After his extremities were badly burned in an open fire, Chrisford required amputations of his arms. Although the teenager had no way to support himself, Chrisford had an encounter that changed his life story.

My friend Ross found him begging on the streets of Lilongwe. Ross shared the good news of grace with the amputee and Chrisford took God up on his kindness. He leaned on God's help, learned to paint with his teeth and toes, and created sketches of Malawians living out their daily lives.

In Chichewa, his native tongue, Chrisford confessed,

> When I lost my hands in the fire, I was devastated. At first, I became angry with God and kept asking why. But God gave me more grace. He helped me see possibilities. Now, because I have no hands, tourists notice my work. God made a way for me to provide for my family.

Giving no credit to himself, Chrisford maintained that grace changed every term in his formula.

- The outcome—both the short and long term.
- How he saw his circumstances.
- Grace equipped, empowered, and energized him to respond.

Defining the Outcome

Chrisford tells others how God's generosity turned his tragedy into something beautiful. Although Chrisford would have never chosen to lose his hands, he now sees God's grander plan for his life. Grace changed his outcome into something meaningful, beneficial, and God-honoring. This could be expressed using mathematical terms.

$$O = H + B + M$$
$$H = God\ Honoring$$
$$B = Beneficial\ for\ Ourselves\ and\ Others$$
$$M = A\ Result\ with\ Meaning\ and\ Purpose$$

Instead of living by explanations, third-level thinkers focus on trust. Although the short-term outcome may be puzzling, the G factor's influence gives assurance that events work out for good. Grace helps us trust the one who holds the outcome rather than fixating on our desired agenda. God moves events toward a meaningful end—sometimes in ways we struggle to understand.

Adverse events leave us disappointed. When things don't turn out as expected, we wonder *why*. We search for a deeper meaning. We can't see how our troubles have any benefit, and we experience a painful disconnect, failing to see any short-term purpose.

$G(C + R) = O$ thinkers understand who's in the center of the universe. They believe God moves situations toward a meaningful outcome.

Sometimes we slip into lower-level thinking. The way we see things turning out doesn't match our mental blueprint. We give God suggestions, telling Him how to do things. And sometimes, we move toward a self-determined outcome opposing God's desired end. Trying to fix things in our own strength, we slip back into self-reliant responses.

We experience disappointments and obsess about why things happen. The loss of a loved one. A financial crisis. Health challenges. A job loss. Conditional acceptance or rejection from those we admire. Fractured relationships. We develop a long list of *why's* and *if only's*.

When a child breaks a toy, the parent knows what the child needs. A child's mind may not understand why it's broken or whether it can be fixed. Wise parents understand children need more than reasons. They need reassurance.

A weary child needs to be embraced and told everything will be all right.

Like a loving parent, God doesn't try to explain things we can't understand. Grace has a better way. Grace reassures us, picks us up, and embraces us. We can only access this kind of comfort and strength through the relational influence of the *G* factor.

Knowing Who Helps with the Whys

During another trip to Malawi, I made an unexpected friend. Henry was a retired truck driver with a worn-out body. In fact, the seventy-year-old had a terminal disease. Henry coughed, walked slowly, and stopped at short intervals. He dragged behind the team and tried to catch his breath. Henry seemed out of place.

I watched him push down dirt trails and share his faith with villagers. I wondered why such a frail man would spend his remaining breaths in a foreign country. One day, we entered a remote village. A crowd gathered under a grove of trees overlooking a soccer field.

After we sang some songs and gave away soccer balls, Henry wiped the sweat off his brow and took a deep breath. "I smoked cigarettes for sixty years and damaged my lungs. Two years ago, I developed lung cancer." He coughed into a handkerchief. "During my treatments, a friend shared with me God's forgiveness and how Jesus took my place on the cross."

He inhaled heavily. "I received God's gift of forgiveness. And you can do the same today." Henry showed the group his blood-stained handkerchief. "I'm going to die soon, but I want to see you in heaven with me. Please don't make mistakes like mine. I've wasted so much of my life. I've missed out on so many things."

Henry sat down on a stool, caught his breath, and continued sharing. I listened and marveled. How did he have the energy to travel halfway across the planet? What could motivate someone to leave the security of his team of doctors? Henry's attitudes and actions can only be explained by unmerited grace working in and through a dying man to accomplish the goals God had purposed.

The *G* factor provides whatever is needed to accomplish the outcome which a wise, powerful, and loving God purposes.

Picture grace as the sun, extending life into the universe. Like the sun's rays, God's kindness emanates from the center. These rays of light give everything needed. Like sunlight, grace flows into our circumstances, affects our responses, and provides what we need to produce the desired outcome.

Our role in the process—a faith response—involves capturing the rays. We receive and make the most of what comes from the source.

The E's Give Everything Needed

The sunlight of grace provides whatever we need to procure a purposeful, God-honoring outcome.

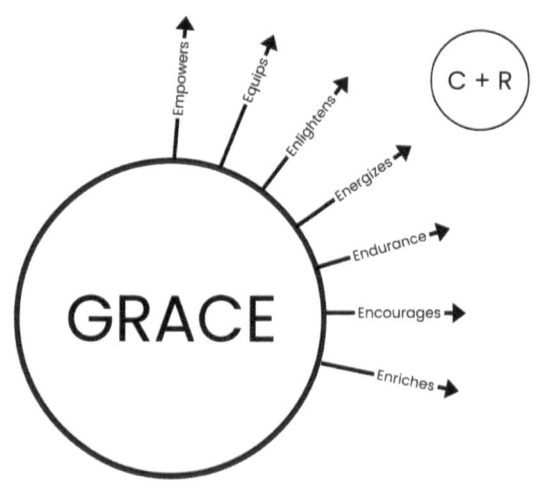

THE E'S GIVE EVERYTHING NEEDED

<u>Grace *empowers*</u>:
Henry and Chrisford both received strength. The *G* factor transformed Chrisford's disability into his ability. Relying on a source greater than himself, Henry could push his worn body down African trails.

The *G* factor worked in their adversities, enhanced their responses, and transformed their life outcomes. Two and two made two hundred. Or maybe two thousand. They received power to turn their weaknesses into strengths.

<u>Undeserved generosity *equips*</u>:
God prepares people for tasks, taking the impossible and making it possible. Chrisford had no idea he could sketch with his teeth until he had no other options. But the provision came through hard work, trial, and error. While Chrisford did his part, God did his.

Henry's cancer gave him credibility. The people in Malawi were more apt to listen to him, knowing he had sacrificed so much to come to share with them. In an unexpected way, his health challenges prepared him to do a task. God's kindness equipped both Henry and Chrisford, transforming their difficulties into opportunities.

<u>The G factor *enlightens*</u>:
How did Henry get the idea of traveling around the world to share his faith? Did a friend encourage him? Or was his crazy notion something on his bucket list, something to check off before he died? Regardless of the way his idea arrived, grace was at work. The *G* factor helped Henry see the value of his story and find ways to connect with others.

For Chrisford, grace introduced the idea of drawing with his teeth. Grace illuminates. It gives ideas, passions, and possibilities to achieve its objectives. When people face a tough decision, the answer may come unexpectedly. A thought appears out of nowhere. A suggestion from a friend. An idea from a book or video. A persistent dream to do something.

In contrast to the second level, where ingenuity originates from the self, creative juices flow from a deeper source for third-level thinkers. Enlightenment comes from

- a Creator who knows individuals better than they know themselves;
- One who knows the blueprint of how, when, and why, things happen;
- a Provider who gives exactly what is needed, always on time;
- a Father who gives all of heaven's resources to faith responders.

Unmerited favor *energizes*:
The *G* factor gave a dying truck driver energy to share his experiences. And the more Henry shared, the more stamina he received. Those who draw on the *G* factor receive vitality to honor God and carry out his plans.

People like Henry, who grasp God's kindness moving through their life events, aren't afraid of expending themselves. They know the more they give, the more grace they receive. The *G* factor increases in proportion to their faith responses. When drained of energy, third-level thinkers go to the source of energy, and generosity flows their way.

Grace gives *endurance*:
What motivated a truck driver with lung cancer to walk down dusty trails? What made Chrisford work hard at his craft? They drew on the *G* factor. God's generosity gave them the strength to keep going.

Perhaps Henry's strength came from knowing he had limited time. Knowing he was close to the finish line, the truck driver made every moment count. Yet, in his circumstances, he learned to lean on grace and receive help.

Chrisford's endurance grew from the need to provide for his family. He persevered because he had no other choice, but grace helped him find a way.

When we feel weak and ready to quit, we're positioned to draw on God's generosity. There, we find the strength to endure difficult situations and setbacks. This supernatural source flows into our natural abilities, giving us hope to endure.

Unearned kindness *encourages*:
I'm sure Chrisford and Henry experienced discouragement when they were overwhelmed by circumstances. The *G* factor gave them courage—in the present—to move forward.

Discouragement plagues us when we don't see our plans coming together. Life's obstacles take the wind out of us. Grace infuses us with the courage to keep going. Sometimes grace arrives in unexpected ways: a listening ear, a compliment, a helping hand, a needed time of rest, contact from an old friend, or someone's reminder of how we make a difference.

Although third-level thinkers face times of despair, they can draw on grace and receive courage.

Grace *enriches*:
The G factor does more than move us toward a purposeful outcome. We receive joy, peace, and contentment along the way, making the journey worthwhile. Grace helps us look beyond the destination and recognize the small things which enrich the journey. We learn to live in the moment and embrace the riches received in the here and now.

Whatever the need, God's generosity abounds and works through our circumstances, providing the means to meet God's objective. The G factor's possibilities are endless.

Unanticipated Outcomes
Jake came to my office for a colonoscopy. "Dr. Chuck, I trust you. Do you remember my father?"

"I'm sorry, but my memory isn't as good as it used to be."

Jake laughed. "Dad had colon cancer, and you fixed him. He lived to be ninety. That's why I came to you."

We scheduled Jake for his colonoscopy. On the day of his procedure, Jake suffered a complication requiring emergency surgery. A routine, minor procedure turned into a major operation.

After surgery, I apologized to Jake and his son. "I did everything right, but everything wrong happened. I apologize things didn't turn out the way we expected."

Jake wiped his eyes and turned his face away. "Doctor, I trusted you."

His son pointed at me. "You're fired. We've called in another surgeon to take over. Dad wants you to leave and never come back."

My mind reeled. How could someone's confidence change so quickly?

Leaving the room, I realized I react in the same way—toward God and others. When something I didn't expect happens, I'm quick to lose faith in God.

When the outcome doesn't match what we expect, how do we respond? Although people and situations may disappoint us, we can't give up on the Great Physician. The one who never gives up on us holds the outcome and has ways of mending what's been broken.

When we watch a movie, we don't stop in the middle—the place where events unravel. We keep watching. We hold on to our expectation things will work out. The tough scenes and challenging events make the movie worthwhile.

When things don't work out the way we anticipate, we shouldn't give up on grace. Broken dreams, unmet expectations, and unfilled longings remind us we are in the middle of the story. Our lives are still unfolding. We haven't reached our destination. We can trust the one who holds the outcome.

- God is not alarmed by what happens.
- God's generosity will not waste a life event.
- God's outcome has purpose and meaning.
- Grace works circumstances toward a story worth telling.

Whatever the short-term brings, we know—in the long run—we win. The *G* factor works in unseen ways to procure a meaningful, favorable, and God-honoring story. Although we might feel like quitting, grace never gives up.

When life isn't turning out the way we expect, we just need to wait. God will remind us the story isn't over. Unmerited favor works through our puzzling difficulties, secures a purposeful outcome, and puts God's generosity on display.

> There are only two types of people in the end: Those who say to God, 'Thy will be done,' and to those to whom God says, in the end, 'Thy will be done.'
>
> C. S. Lewis

CHAPTER TWELVE

Wally, an Old Table, and a Doorkeeper
Wally swallowed an open safety pin. The pin lodged in his intestines and damaged his bowels. After removing the diseased bowel, I headed to the waiting room to find Wally's family. His mother, Lexi, sat in the lobby sewing a pair of green socks.

She shook her head as she stitched. "If he doesn't get his Lithium, he'll go crazy. Wally's not right in the head. I should know. I've been his momma for thirty years." She pulled another green thread through the sock and continued. "If Wally doesn't get his medicine, he's hard to control. He does crazy things. But I guess he's your problem now. I'm going home to rest. I'll be back in a couple of days to pick him up."

"It will be a couple of days before he can take his psychiatric medications," I said. "I'll let the hospitalist know."

"Okay," Lexi said. "Don't say I didn't warn you."

"Miss Lexi, you sew pretty well. Have you ever thought about helping in the OR?"

Lexi laughed. "Tell ya what. Let's make a trade. If you take Wally, I'll come and help."

Where's Wally?
At two in the morning, six hours after surgery, I received a phone call from the hospital administrator. "Doctor, your patient's room is empty. Security searched the hospital grounds and can't locate him. We've called the police."

"Okay, call me when you find him." I rolled over and went back to sleep.

Two hours later, I received another call from the nursing supervisor. "Doctor, they found Wally. He pushed his IV pole across the street, went into a department store, and grabbed some orange sneakers and sodas." She giggled. "He walked up to the cash register with his rear anatomy exposed for the midnight shoppers."

"So, they called the hospital?" "No," the nurse said. "They called the police, and the officers brought him back to the hospital."

"What did they do with the IV pole?"

"They shoved it in the trunk of the police car. And guess what? They gave him the sodas and the shoes."

I turned over in bed. "Well, thanks for the update."

"Wait, don't hang up," the nurse said. "He didn't pull out his nose hose. Can I put it back to suction?"

"Yep," I replied. "Low continuous wall suction."

"Can he have his soda?"

"It's four in the morning. Handle it." I groaned.

The following day, I walked into Wally's room. Wally had pulled the covers over his head, exposing his new orange sneakers. I pulled the sheet off his face. He smiled and pointed to his shoes, tapping his toes together.

"Wally, I heard you had quite an adventure last night. I was with you, in spirit, I guess. They gave me updates on your whereabouts every five minutes." My sarcasm went over Wally's head.

He gulped one of his sodas and laughed, grabbing his nose-hose. "Watch this."

Wally swallowed again, crossed his eyes, and fixated on the tube taped to his nose. "Wait for it," he said. His nose hose shook.

A couple of seconds later, soda came up through the tube. Wally giggled. "See, it goes down and then comes right back up."

"Yep. Cause and effect. You swallow fluid down, and then the tube sucks it out of your stomach. It's amazing."

Later that afternoon, the day nurse called. "Your patient pulled out the tube in his nose. He's drinking soda. Can we expedite his discharge?"

Wally had worn out his welcome. Deciding he was safer with Lexi, we gave him Lithium and sent him home.

A Dose of Favor

Many people picture grace as medicine. After a spoonful, burdens turn into blessings. Reality suggests things aren't so simple. No medications solve all of life's problems. No tablets wrap everything in a bow.

In Wally's case, bittersweet happenings brought both laughter and tears. Other, more tragic experiences leave us puzzled, frustrated, and bitter.

The *G* factor gives more than a dose of self-help and irrational positivity. God's favor helps by transforming our minds. Embracing grace changes the way we think. We may not always understand what happens, but we know who holds the future. God promises not to waste our troubles.

Grace has no "gotcha" moments. God doesn't yank our chain to pull us through adversity without a purpose. God's generosity helps us cry with hope, laugh at ourselves, and trust in a beneficial outcome.

Grace Influences Our Circumstances

In the previous chapter's story, Jake lost trust in his doctor. He only believed in the skill of his physician provided the outcome matched his expectations. On the third level, trust takes on a new meaning. We pray and hope for a specific outcome, but we trust the one who holds the outcome even when things happen which we don't understand.

We rely on grace to bring us through. The *G* factor begins by transforming the way we see adversity. The life equation can be tweaked to visualize the *G* factor's influence on our life events.

$$GC + GR = O$$

G influences C in two ways. God can change the circumstances. Grace delivers. Adding a supernatural element to the equation opens the possibility of miracles.

Although a materialist believes miracles are impossible, grace thinkers see supernatural possibilities. Materialists see the universe as a closed box where cause and effect cannot be influenced. Grace thinkers leave the box open. They believe God can place his hand in the box and interfere.

Since God can make something out of nothing, intervening in events becomes possible. The cause-effect box remains open. And God, the maker of the box, can interrupt life's chain of events. He can put his hand in the box at any point.

Although God can intervene using the miraculous, he tends to use a second method. Adversity becomes the means of personal transformation.

God doesn't always bring us *out* of our challenges. Grace brings us *through* them. Instead of changing our circumstances, God performs a greater miracle: a changed life. God's love helps us grow, using our troubles to change the way we see ourselves, others, and life itself.

Opportunities for Growth
Grace used the loss of Chrisford's hands to help him develop new skills. The amputee's challenges forced him to learn new things and to develop unique abilities. On the third level, God doesn't do things *to* us. Grace does things *for* us, working through circumstances in a beneficial way.

Christians never fail tests. God's generosity lets them repeat the trial repeatedly until they pass. Concerned with more than the short-term outcome, grace designs the test to help us grow in character.

Opportunities to Relate to God
When I walked with Henry down dusty African trails, I noticed something. God's witness was evident in Henry's life. Henry's cancer brought him into greater intimacy with God. For Henry, God was real and present, helping him through his sickness.

When a Christian goes through adversity, God's presence feels palpable. The *G* factor surfaces in tangible ways, assuring a grace thinker. In times of need, God's present help shows up. Grace helps us recognize the possibilities in our problems.

We see opportunities to experience God in new ways through life's challenges. On the third level, adversity encourages grace responders to depend on and draw on God's help in troubles.

Opportunities to Impact Others
Difficulties are the soil where influence grows. When people see our affliction, they become curious. They are drawn to our troubles. They are more apt to listen and learn. Watchers want to know how we are pulling through our trials. When bystanders see us respond in extraordinary ways, they perceive the presence of another element.

Adversity draws attention to third-level responses.

OPPORTUNITIES TO IMPACT OTHERS

Through my mother, Linda, I witnessed firsthand how grace changes the way we see things.

In 2014, my mother developed a dry cough. She went to her doctor, who started her on antibiotics. Despite treatment, her cough persisted. CT scans and more invasive studies were ordered. All were normal.

Linda went about her business, working in her floral shop, dismissing her symptoms. Over the next two years, her breathing worsened. Eventually, she was diagnosed with a rare kind of lung cancer.

No one expected my mother to have lung cancer. She had never touched a cigarette. Her cancer was unique. We watched her wither as the tumor and the chemotherapy slowly sucked the life out of her.

The time came for friends and well-wishers to visit and give mom their last respects.

One afternoon she said, "Come on. I have something to show you."

We went to an old shed stuffed with collectibles—mainly floral decorations and items mom used in her business. Mom told me what to do with her treasures, giving specific instructions about every item.

I trudged along, carrying mom's oxygen machine, trying to sound interested, and wondering why all this mattered. Mom stopped and caught her breath every minute or so. She rummaged through items and moved slowly through the shed. At the back of the barn, Mom sat down in an old rocking chair.

I turned up the oxygen and sighed. "Mom, I don't get it. Aren't there more important things we could be doing?"

My mom coughed and pointed to a piece of furniture covered by a blanket. Her shallow breathing slowed, and her face lit up. She whispered, "This is the reason I brought you here."

I pulled the sheet away, expecting to see something magical. Instead, I groaned in disbelief. I had exposed an old table made of post oak. One-by-twelve boards were nailed over its rickety frame. The old boards were smooth and worn. At best, the table might be useful for firewood.

Disappointed, I looked back at my mother. Tears rolled down her cheeks. I didn't know what to say. For a moment, I thought the chemotherapy had gotten the best of her. Before I could speak, my mother told her story.

"This was Papa Roscoe's and Georgia's kitchen table. I remember us sitting around it when I was a child. Your great-grandfather made it for them on their wedding day."

My mother rocked in her chair and reminisced about old times. The longer I listened, the more I understood her intentions. My mother shared memories of being raised around that old rickety table.

In her dying breaths, she impacted my life by seizing the opportunity to impart things of value. And at that moment, she had my full attention.

Mom's intentional moment made an impact. She used her cancer to influence me and others in meaningful ways. Her story helped me see the hidden value of things. In sharing her memories, she imparted value and life lessons through a beaten-up table.

My mother wasn't a Bible Thumper. She didn't fit in with the "believe and don't ask questions" group. But in the last years of her life, Mom took hold of grace. Or perhaps grace took hold of her.

Watching how my mother suffered and how she used her cancer to influence others helped me grow up and see things through a different set of lenses. I learned to trust God even when the outcome didn't fit my mental formula. In my mother, I saw the presence of God demonstrated in a real way.

The Rest of Nick's Story

In chapter seven, I introduced Nick. After divorcing his mother, Nick's dad hid him away in an orphanage. After his dad remarried, Nick came back and lived with his family. Nick's dad and stepmom forced him to hide the family secret. The preacher's son couldn't tell people about his birth mother, the orphanage, or his dad's divorce and remarriage. Bound to live a lie, Nick finally had enough.

Nick left his dad and the ministry he never wanted. He went on a long quest to find his mother—and himself. After many years, Nick found his mother in Houston and moved to be closer to her.

In his fifties, Nick suffered a stroke, leaving him with a speech impediment. Through his circumstances, Nick began a long journey back to God. Now he greets people at the church door and welcomes them in. Because

THE REST OF NICK'S STORY

of his stroke, Nick's words get mangled. His church-door conversations are short and abrupt.

When I see Nick at the church door, I wonder what would happen if people knew his story. Perhaps they would pause before they entered and ponder whether they needed another sermon.

Nick's desire to stand at the door, offer a handshake, and usher people inside was a lifetime in the making. Nick overcame his emotional barriers and learned to see his past through new lenses. God's generosity helped Nick find himself, God, his family, and his purpose. Grace brought him full circle.

The *G* factor helps us see our situations from a new perspective.

- We learn to laugh at ourselves and at life's funny happenings.
- We come to trust an all-loving, all-wise God.
- Our painful past wounds become platforms for our growth and healing.
- Undeserved kindness turns old tables into heirlooms and illness into opportunities.

God's favor reminds us how our story weaves into a grander one, where burdens become blessings.

Grace transforms our circumstances, moving them toward a meaningful outcome. *G* times *C*. We cannot minimize the other term the *G* factor influences—our personal response. Our role involves receiving, drawing, asking, seeking, and finding grace in our life events.

Grace should amaze us. It infuses strength and an ability to do—with God's help—what we could not do through our self-responses. Next, we'll explore how to recognize our level of thinking.

Conquered

*Out of the light that dazzles me
Bright as the sun from pole to pole,
I thank the God I know to be,
For Christ—the Conqueror of my soul.*

*Since His, the sway of circumstance,
I would not wince nor cry aloud.
Under the rule which men call chance,
My head, with joy, is humbly bowed.*

*Beyond this place of sin and tears,
That Life with Him and His, the aid,
That, spite the menace of the years,
Keeps, and will keep me unafraid.*

*I have no fear though straight the gate
He cleared from punishment the scroll.
Christ is the Master of my fate!
Christ is the Captain of my soul!*

Dorothy Day

CHAPTER THIRTEEN

Elliot and the Baggage Carrier

Dorothy Day's poem *Conquered* reflects the paradigm shift we can experience by moving to a God-centered framework. Day frames a third-level response to Henley's *Invictus*. In her interpretation, grace changes everything. Self moves to the periphery and God dwells in the center. When we realize the infinite potential of the *G* factor and draw on its resources, we no longer see ourselves as victims, heroes, or zeroes.

In high school, Elliot was a blue-chip offensive tackle. He won several awards in football and went on to play in college. After he finished college, Elliot's lifestyle was no longer active, but he maintained his daily consumption of calories. In fifteen years, Elliot gained over one hundred and fifty pounds.

Now forty, Elliot was hospitalized because of severe sleep apnea. He was then transferred to the nursing home on a ventilator. He came to my office with a tube in his windpipe—a tracheostomy—and used a portable machine to move air through his lungs. To speak, Elliot had to remove the tube from his windpipe, close the hole with his finger, and push air through his vocal cords.

"Doctor, I need help. I can't do this on my own. I've tried everything. Low-carb, Paleo, and Atkins. I'm desperate. Can you help me?"

I looked at Elliot's chart. He weighed four hundred pounds and had all the symptoms which result from obesity: diabetes, sleep apnea, hypertension, and arthritis.

"Elliot, you're just too big and at too great a risk to have surgery in a rural hospital. Let me send you to Houston. Heck, they do a TV show down there with guys like you."

"I've already tried, Doc. They won't take Medicaid."

I paused and changed the subject. "So, Elliot, why do you want to pursue weight loss surgery? It's risky. And why me? We don't have the resources. I'm a country surgeon. It only takes one operation to get me thrown out of town. Let's get you to a place more equipped to handle your problems."

Elliot placed the tubing back on his tracheostomy and bowed his head. When I turned to leave, Elliot removed the tubing again and pointed to the machine. "Help me. I'm trapped. I am so tired of living this way. I've tried to change, but I can't do it on my own."

Elliot's choices had strapped him on an emotional roller coaster. When he lost weight, he saw himself as the hero. And when failure followed, he moved into the $C + r = O$ way of thinking.

I wondered whether Elliot pictured himself through the $C = O$ equation. Did he want me to come in, be the hero, fix his problem and alter his outcome?

What if I failed? Would Elliot pull out his victim card and blame me for a less than optimal outcome? In the past, I had been burned when things didn't turn out the way people expected. In those instances, lots of fingers were pointed in my direction, questioning the adequacy of my responses.

On the other hand, maybe I was the one wearing victim lenses. Could I be making excuses, desiring to shift responsibility to another surgeon?

Elliot gave me a fist bump on his way down the hall. "It's okay. I understand. God will help me find a way." Another option crossed my mind. I could encourage Elliot to make minor adjustments, begin to prepare him for surgery, and call some colleagues. Although I couldn't fix all of Elliot's problems, perhaps I could be a small part of his solution.

"Elliot, come back, and we'll start the process. It may take six months to move you through all the paperwork. We'll see what happens."

Everyone faces life events which require us to choose a course of action. The filter we use to view them affects the outcome. Lots of equations were running through my mind as I thought about Elliot. And from Elliot's comments, I knew he viewed things through several lenses.

Determining Our Level

Grace is available to draw on. Asking for help begins with thinking about the lenses through which we see our life events. When facing situations, we can ask ourselves questions.

- Which set of lenses am I using?
- Through what formula or level do I process life events?
- What gear am I shifting into?

If only the mind easily shifted into higher gears like an automatic transmission. This mental shift doesn't happen automatically. It requires intentionality.

To shift gears in a vehicle with a standard transmission, the driver must push on the clutch. Think of the above questions as a mental clutch. Before placing the vehicle in gear, we should shift our minds into neutral. When we face a circumstance, we can pause, push in our mental clutch, and notice our level of thinking.

In this process, we can ask ourselves questions to assess our level and determine our mental gear. Before we respond, we can pause to ponder our choices and consider the formula which dominates our thinking. This gives us the opportunity to shift into grace gear.

Who's in Control?

Our awareness of who's in charge depends on our formula. Third-level thinkers have a unique view of reality. Without minimizing their responsibility, they believe God is in control.

My friend Marcus called me after Thanksgiving. "Hey, Buddy, hope you had a good Turkey Day."

"How's your family?" I asked.

"Good," he said. "We lost my dad last summer to COVID. My son, Will, took it hard."

"Is he still in college?"

"Yep. And he didn't come home last Thanksgiving." Marcus paused. "Will and I had a long talk about his grandpa. He carried a lot of guilt. You wouldn't believe what he told me today. Will said, 'Dad, I didn't come home last Thanksgiving to protect Grandpa. I didn't want him to get infected, but Grandpa got COVID anyway. And I never got to see him again. I feel bad because I didn't come home last Thanksgiving.'"

Will had learned a lesson the hard way. We are not in control.

When the accounts of Jesus's crucifixion are examined, we may begin to wonder who was in charge.

Appearances can be deceiving. On one level, Jesus's trial seemed to be controlled by the Jewish leaders and by the Romans. Pilate, being the Roman governor, had the final say. He had the power to change the outcome—or so it seems.

Peter, Jesus's disciple, thought he could be the hero. He took up a sword to save Jesus from his enemies. Through his inadequate responses, Peter learned he wasn't in charge.

Some perceive Jesus was playing the victim or the zero. He could have mustered a strong response, stood up for himself, opposed the religious rulers, and justified himself before Pilate. Looking through this lens, people see Jesus's trial as unfair, even puzzling.

Although things appeared to be out of Jesus's hands, they weren't. Third-level thinkers see God's generosity in the crucifixion events. God was working behind the scenes, creating a positive outcome—one which defies human understanding, one beneficial to humankind.

Humanly speaking, control is an illusion. We are not in charge.

Will didn't have to carry the whole burden of his grandfather's health on his shoulders. He had the opportunity to see the situation through grace lenses. God was in control. When facing challenges, we can put our mental clutch in neutral and ask ourselves a question: "am I aware of who's in charge of my circumstances?"

Where's the Focus?
Our focus determines our future. And the elements of the equation which we prioritize have a profound effect on our level of thinking.

To motivate his sales team, a manager stood up in a meeting and displayed a large piece of white paperboard. With a pen, he placed a small black dot in the middle of the board and asked, "What do you see?"

WHERE'S THE FOCUS?

The group members answered, each making elaborate descriptions of the dot.

One salesman interrupted. "I see the dot, but I see something else. I see the whiteboard—the background where the dot is placed."

This individual saw something the others didn't see. He focused on the bigger picture. He saw the dot in relation to the board. The *G* factor helps us see our circumstances and responses in light of a bigger picture.

Victims magnify their life events.

$$C = O$$

Zeroes focus on their weaknesses.

$$C + r = O$$

Heroes glorify their adequate responses.

$$C + R = O$$

Although grace thinkers see the second level, they see a bigger picture. Like the perceptive salesman, they see the dot $C + R = O$, and they picture this dot centered in the big whiteboard of God's helpful responses: $G(C + R) = O$.

Lenses	Victim	Hero/Zero	Grace
Focus	C	R or r	G

When facing circumstances, we can stop, question ourselves, and consider which element we prioritize. If we dwell on life challenges, we may see ourselves as victims. When we focus solely on the R term, we may be the hero of our story. Fixing our attention on God's grace changes our focus to ask, "how can I cooperate with God and draw on grace?"

Equation	Focus	Attitude
$C = O$	Change the circumstance	Self-entitled
$C + r = O$	Inadequate performance	Self-destructive
$C + R = O$	Enhancing performance	Self-reliance
$G(C + R) = O$	Draw on grace/Cooperate	Gratitude

Who Gets the Credit?

On the lower levels, people tend to point fingers and play the shame-and-blame game. Some categorize people as heroes or zeroes. Third-level thinkers have a different viewpoint, a better way to see themselves and others.

Adding the *G* factor into their thinking helps them realize everybody needs God's help. On the third level, fingers don't point outward—they point upward. God serves as the hero. Then, grace thinkers point inward, asking how their responses reflect generosity toward others.

I bought into the shame-and-blame game on my first visit with Elliot. Concerned about being blamed for bad outcomes, I feared doing anything. I had the hero/zero state of mind. I should have viewed our interaction as an opportunity to put God on display.

On the third level, thinkers move beyond asking which person receives the credit and who gets the blame. The life equation changes the direction of our fingers—upward. Asking who gets the credit for the outcome helps us become aware of our level of thinking.

Who Carries the Burden?

$G(C+R) = O$ thinkers adopt a unique perspective regarding responsibility. Since God controls the outcome and should receive the credit, Christians see life as a joint venture, one of cooperation. Attitudes and actions aren't trivialized. They are seen through God's generosity.

On the third level, God has the most significant part of the equation. He moves events toward a meaningful purpose. Grace thinkers focus on how to adjust and cooperate. They draw on grace to enhance their responses.

My son Jonathan graduated from high school and moved to Chicago to study linguistics. We knew he would experience culture shock after being raised in a small town. Wanting to set out on his own, Jonathan rejected our offer to come along and help.

Without his knowledge, we arrived in Chicago before he did. We booked a hotel, hid out, and followed Jonathan from afar. We gave him enough rope to grow—but not enough to hang himself.

WHO CARRIES THE BURDEN?

From the moment Jonathan stepped off the train, he was unprepared for his experiences. Jonathan had no money for a taxi, so he hauled his luggage through the streets, asking disinterested people for directions.

Overwhelmed, he finally called Mom and Dad, unaware we were just around the corner. I came out of hiding and waved at my son. "Jon, look over your shoulder."

Jonathan was relieved to see his parents (or at least a familiar face). We called a cab and took his bags to his dormitory.

Level	Who's Responsible	Attitude	Response
First	Others	Deflect burdens	Shift responsibility
Second	Self	Carry burdens	Self-performance
Third	God + Self	Release burdens	Cooperation

Baggage, burdens, and responsibilities weigh each of us down. The *G* factor reminds us that our heavenly Father is there, closer than we think, ready to help with the load, waiting for us to ask.

- Victims want someone else to carry the bags for them.
- Heroes carry their burdens with self-effort and self-reliance.
- Zeroes carry their burden of guilt and regret.

When our circumstances place heavy burdens on our shoulders, we can stop and ask ourselves two questions:

- Who's responsible?
- How much of the burden should I carry?

Shirley was a patient who became a family friend. She carried many burdens. Her poor choices led to divorce early in life. Working two jobs, Shirley provided for her daughter, Beth Anne.

Rebelling against her mother's advice, Beth Anne began dating. Like her mother, she chose poorly. Watching her daughter repeat her mistakes broke Shirley's heart. Because of her own relational baggage and her own mistakes, Shirley felt inadequate to counsel her daughter. Shirley couldn't sleep. She began to drink and have outbursts of anger.

Shirley expressed her concerns to Beth Anne, but her encouragement fell on deaf ears. Shirley blamed herself, saying, "Like mother, like daughter."

Shirley's past, coupled with Beth Anne's relational choices, left her feeling guilty, anxious, and responsible for her daughter's decisions. Shirley's burdens were too much to carry. My wife Joanna reminded Shirley of her opportunities.

Shirley could step into the third level of thinking by asking herself, *who's responsible*? She could step into freedom by accepting God's forgiveness.

With her past behind her, Shirley could let God carry the baggage. And who knows? If Shirley factored grace into her thinking, her past messes could serve as a well of wisdom for Beth Anne.

Looking at her circumstances through grace lenses, Shirley could:

- Be honest with Beth Anne about her failures, mistakes, and poor choices.
- Draw on God's resources for help in situations similar to past failures.
- Remind herself of Beth Anne's responsibility.

Shirley's zero mindset could be considered a good starting place. When we come to the end of ourselves and recognize our helplessness, we only have one place to go for help: God's generosity. Grace's sufficiency will carry the bags if we choose to release them.

We've explored three questions to help us consider our mental formula.

- Who's in control?
- Who gets the credit?
- Who carries the burden?

Questions seem to beget more questions. In the next chapter, we'll discuss more interrogatives to help us discover how we process events. And we'll learn how Elliot's desperation led him to a power greater than his own.

Spiritual strength is quite different. It is identified neither with the politics of strength nor with those of weakness. Whether the conflict is between husband and wife, between two competitors, or between nations, spiritual strength provides a way of escape from the tragic dilemma ... It introduces a new element, a new dimension, into human affairs. It acts on a different level: no longer on men's power relationships, but on their very nature. And by changing their nature it changes the premises of the problem.

Paul Tournier

CHAPTER FOURTEEN

Significant or Special?

In the last chapter, we evaluated which formula we use to process our life events. Here are four more questions which can heighten our awareness:

- From what level do we draw self-esteem?
- Are we feeling stressed and burdened?
- What do we fear?
- What language are we using?

Previously, we met Elliot, the former athlete who had come to the end of himself. Elliot later returned to my office, unable to find someone else to perform his weight loss surgery.

Elliot smiled and gave me a fist bump. "I've lost eighteen pounds."

I patted Elliot on the back. "That's great. How are you doing it? Are you exercising?"

Elliot raised his hands. "Yes, I'm exercising. But change starts in your heart, goes to your mind, and then moves through your body."

"What do you mean?" I asked.

"When I was younger, I thought I was special. I was on my way to the pros. And then I hurt my knee. I placed all my value in being an athlete. And when I was injured, I lost myself." He took a whiff on his breathing machine. "Max has been coming to the nursing home. Now he's a preacher, but back in the day, he was a football coach. He talked to me about how God sees me. Do you know what he said?

I leaned forward. "What did he say?"

"He said, 'Elliot, you're not special. You are significant.' When Max said those words, a light bulb turned on in my brain. I had based my worth upon how well I could block and tackle. Back when I played football, I thought I was special. Well, I'm not special anymore, but I can be significant. I can make a difference now, even in the nursing home. Every morning, I get up and push old people down the hall. That's how I'm shuckin' weight. At first, the old folks were scared of me. Imagine having a three-hundred and fifty-pound tackle push you down the hall." Elliot laughed. "Doc, I give them the ride of their life. I push their wheelchair, and they carry my breathing machine. I'm making a difference."

"Elliot, that's great," I said. "But isn't it difficult with your lung condition?"

"Not with God's help. When you are a man of significance, you find a way."

Formula	Weak or Strong	Lens	Type of Response
$C + r = O$	Natural weakness	Zero	Inadequate responses
$C + R = O$	Natural Strength	Hero	Adequate responses
$G(C + R) = O$	Spiritual Strength/ Natural Weakness	Grace	Adequately inadequate responses

Grace enlightened and empowered Elliot. Transformed by his significant purpose, Elliot changed his thinking. Max's encouragement helped Elliot see himself through different lenses. He learned to base his value on God's generosity, not on his own performance.

Paul Tournier, a psychiatrist and third-level thinker, described the levels as strong and weak. Heroes draw strength from themselves and perceive their responses as sufficient. Zeroes, possessing weak responses, realize their inadequacy to meet life's challenges.

Grace thinkers view themselves through a different grid.

In one sense, they consider themselves a zero, but they respond to their insufficiency by tapping into the G factor's power. They appropriate the resources God gives to help them through their life events.

Instead of depending upon their own adequacy, $G(C + R) = O$ thinkers draw upon the sufficiency of grace.

Assessing the Source of Our Esteem

The way we measure our self-worth influences our life's outcome. Every thought level evaluates personal value through different lenses. Victims determine their worth by association, drawing on others for their esteem. $C = O$ thinkers want to identify themselves with heroes and, if possible, avoid zeroes. In a sense, their esteem is dictated by how others have treated them.

Those who abide on the $C + r = O$ level adopt a poor self-image. Like Elliot before his breakthrough, zeroes undervalue themselves. They have trouble making decisions. They lose confidence. Zeroes often struggle with anxiety, depression, addictions, and relationships.

Second-level psychology attempts to elevate low self-esteem by nurturing self-belief and promoting self-worth. Some counselors employ self-talk and meditation to transform zeroes into heroes. Without tapping into grace, many counselors may neglect the most significant source of emotional power. This doesn't mean self-help techniques aren't effective, but they are self-limited. They minimize or exclude the G factor's work.

On the lower levels, transforming power must come from within, and some people don't have the resiliency to make healthy changes.

Many victims have experienced horrific life events: rape, incest, abandonment, betrayal, and all kinds of social injustices. They do not have the power within themselves to elevate their esteem with healthier approaches. The same goes for zeroes. Many are overwhelmed by life events. They dwell on the guilt of past mistakes, fear the future, and don't possess the strength to view themselves as people of value.

Whatever techniques are used—shock treatments, medications, counseling, cognitive behavioral therapy—many individuals don't have the power to change. Low self-esteem paralyzes them and prevents them from living up to their potential.

The transformational power of grace influences our self-image. Elliot first had to adjust how he saw himself by viewing his life through God's eyes.

How Does God See Us?

In God's eyes, our natural responses will never be adequate. We are not special, and sometimes we are our own worst enemy. Our desire to place ourselves in the center separates us from God. Here's the good news: the third level explains how God responds on our behalf.

When we are powerless to change ourselves, God intervenes—doing for us what we cannot do in our own strength. This gives real hope for victims and zeroes.

In God's estimation,

- We aren't mere cosmic accidents. Our lives have a purpose.
- We are made in God's image and have immense value.
- Our circumstances are opportunities wrapped in grace.
- We have the possibility to live free of guilt and regret.
- We have an objective reason to be optimistic.
- We are individuals to be loved.

Since God's generosity forgives our past, secures our present, and determines our future, we have hope. Our optimism embeds itself in a simple reality. We see ourselves, our responses, our events, and our identity through God's lenses—not our own. Our self-assessment should consider the question, "from what level do I draw my self-esteem?"

Esteeming Others More Than Ourselves
Bernice pointed her finger at me when I walked into the exam room. "I'm not here for a lecture. I'm here to get a biopsy."

Feeling awkward, I first acknowledged her daughter, then asked Bernice, "Okay, how can I help you?"

Bernice removed her shirt. A large breast tumor had eroded through the skin. She had placed gauze over open wounds to catch the drainage. The tumor, now grown into her ribs and muscles, was too large to be removed.

I stepped back. "Why now?"

Bernice said, "I'm here to have genetic testing. I want my daughters to know if they are at risk for cancer. I don't want them to suffer like I have."

"How long have you had breast cancer?"

Her daughter, Arely, answered. "Fourteen years. She's seen lots of surgeons and oncologists. Every time she sees a new doctor, they scold her for not getting treated."

I exhaled. "Well, Bernice, you've survived fourteen years with postmenopausal breast cancer. People can also die from surgery and chemo."

ESTEEMING OTHERS MORE THAN OURSELVES

Bernice gave a thumbs up. "Yep."

Arely said, "Mom was diagnosed with breast cancer when we were young, but Dad had Alzheimer's, and Mom was Dad's caregiver."

Bernice put her shirt back on. "And we had no insurance. They sent me to an indigent hospital, but we made too much money to meet their criteria for charity."

Arely put her arm around Bernice. "Mom held the family together."

I nodded. "I see. Well, I'll schedule a biopsy."

The door opened. An adult man with Down's Syndrome entered the room. He hugged Bernice and looked at me. "Are you being nice to my mother?"

"Yes," I said.

Equation	Focus of Esteem	Source of Image	Personal Esteem
$C = O$	Uncertain Esteem	Image defined by others	Devalue
$C + r = O$	Self-esteem	Self-defined image	Undervalue
$C + R = O$	Inflated Esteem	Self-defined image	Overvalue
$G(C + R) = O$	Grace's Esteem	God-defined image	God, then others, then self

"I thank God for Mommy. She's the best. She prays with me and reads me stories. Mommy has always been there for us."

I left the room piecing together Bernice's life story. Initially, I thought Bernice had low self-esteem and felt unworthy of having her cancer treated. Quite the opposite.

Bernice didn't undervalue herself—she wasn't thinking about herself at all. She had a husband with Alzheimer's, a son with Down's Syndrome, and two other young children who needed her attention.

On the lower levels, the search for self-esteem can digress into self-absorption. Grace makes possible a radically different life. God's generosity helps us rise above our self-centeredness. We learn to put our esteem in a larger context, in which others are valued more than ourselves.

$G\ (C + R) = O$ thinkers consider how to honor others, encourage them, and find ways to build up their confidence. Both Elliot and Bernice learned the value of being significant in God's eyes. This was expressed by esteeming others more than themselves.

When we face life challenges, we can stop and ask ourselves:

- How does God see me in this circumstance?
- From what level do I draw my esteem?
- Am I drawing self-worth from myself, others, or God?
- What am I doing to encourage others?
- Where do I fit in relation to God and others?

What am I feeling?
I have a 1972 Chevy named Ole Blue. The old truck has lots of nuances. One involves the gears. Ole Blue has no gear indicator. The transmission has been replaced several times. To know Ole Blue's gear, the driver must count clicks when shifting through the gears and listen to the engine.

If the engine hums and purrs like a kitten, you're in the right gear. When the truck screams and roars like an angry lion, a gentle nudge on the gear stick will shift it back into place.

Unlike new cars, Ole Blue doesn't have flashing indicator lights. The driver must listen, feel, and be aware of the engine. Lack of mindfulness can cause costly consequences.

I let my wife Joanna drive Ole Blue—once. She wasn't aware of the minor quirks.

I followed behind Joanna for twenty minutes. We cruised down the highway at sixty miles per hour. Suddenly, smoke began to rise from the hood. Joanna pulled to the roadside. Ole Blue's engine sputtered and died. The overheated engine had burned out.

Why did Ole Blue's engine burn up? The truck had been running in second gear.

In some ways, our lives are like car engines. We are designed to operate in specific gears. If we operate in the wrong gear, our engine experiences wear and tear and eventually burns out.

WHAT AM I FEELING?

Often, we drive through life in lower gears, unaware of the stress on our mental engine. Developing an awareness of our brain function formula helps us make the shift. When we listen and adjust gears, life works better. Periodically, we should ask ourselves:

- Does my mental engine show signs of stress and burnout?
- What am I feeling?
- Am I listening to my mental and emotional engine?

The victim gear, in which somebody else carries the load, has stressors.

Victims often feel angry about their circumstances and frustrated because they have been disappointed by their heroes. Zeroes feel the tension of driving in second gear. They are aware their engine is overheating but feel helpless to change their situation.

The engine of a $C + R = O$ thinker feels a different kind of stress. In chapter five, we explored how heroes worry about failure and fear exposure. Afraid of being perceived as a zero, they expend tons of energy, justify their decisions, and protect their image.

Shifting into grace gear allows our mental engines to operate in the way they were fashioned. In third gear, God carries the burden and determines the outcomes. Why strive and suffer burnout in a lower gear?

Our engine functions more efficiently when we adjust our attitude, acknowledge God's control, and cooperate with what God is doing in our life events. Third gear thinkers have the potential to experience freedom.

- We don't have to be angry and frustrated with failure.
- We're not helpless. We have the freedom to cooperate with God.
- We have nothing to hide. We are free from the fear of failure.
- We can enjoy relationships, be ourselves, and enjoy emotional intimacy.
- We can experience peace and joy in our circumstances.

Of course, we never fully reach the plateau. Even when we operate in our spiritual gear, the natural ones are still operational. When third-level thinkers slip into lower gears, they always have access to the *G* factor. We can shift into third gear and tap into God's unmerited favor.

Our mental engines were not designed to carry certain burdens. Understanding how grace works—in our failures, successes, and all the in-between responses—begins with awareness. When we experience life challenges, we can assess our gear, listen to our emotional engine, and ask ourselves, "what am I feeling?"

Gear	Who's responsible	Indicators
Victim	Others	Anger/Frustration
Zero	Self	Helplessness/Inadequacy
Hero	Self	Fear/Stress/Isolation
Grace	God	Freedom/Peace/Joy

What Do We Fear?

Every gear or level experiences some type of fear. The *G* factor introduces a contrite attitude into the minds of third-level thinkers. Trepidation in a God-centered framework looks different.

- The fear of missing out on the joys of cooperation with God.
- The dread of suffering consequences of poor choices.
- The anxiety of not living up to one's God-given potential.

Those seeing through grace lenses have nothing to dread. They can express failures openly, recognizing they are not the story's hero.

Formula	Source of fear	Survival tactics
Victim	Dread Loss of Hero	Build/Destroy Pedestals
Hero	Exposure/Failure/Loss of Credibility	Hide Failures/Play the Fame, Shame and Blame
Grace	Missing God's Outcome	Draw on Grace & Cooperate

Those who participate with the $G(C + R) = O$ mindset do not need to hide their deficiencies, isolate themselves, or deflect the blame. When failure comes, they can be honest with themselves, others, and God.

- The outcome of events doesn't depend solely upon our efforts.

- God's favor moves things forward, sometimes in spite of ourselves.
- When we cooperate with God, He takes full responsibility for the outcome.

Third-level thinkers trust God's generosity to take failures, reshape them, and move things toward a purposeful outcome. This confidence is a faith response, a growing awareness that God will receive credit.

Listening to Our Language

Our words embody the thoughts and ideas in our minds. Developing an awareness of our words provides a valuable insight into our level of thinking.

Frank had many positive qualities and was considered an ideal worker. He was creative, worked long hours, and was resourceful. Frank had a downfall. He didn't play well with others. He thought he was the only employee giving one hundred percent on the job. Frank often said, "If I don't do the paperwork, then no one does it."

Quick to blame others, Frank struggled with team projects. He made statements like, "They steal every idea I bring to the table," or "I can't trust their shoddy work." What was Frank's favorite expression? *I*.

Frank could learn a lot by listening to his own language. And so could we. If our words truly express our thoughts, we should often examine them. Think of some of the phrases used in previous chapters. The $C = O$ thinkers used victim talk.

- "All I need is a good doctor to fix the blockages." —*Hector*
- "I'm fat. I need to lose twenty more pounds." —*Brandy*
- "I was a misfit." —*Tonya*

Some used zero expressions.

- "My world is falling apart." —*Joan*
- "Like mother, like daughter." —*Shirley*

Others expressed $C + R = O$ attitudes:

- "Don't feel sorry for me. I'm fine." —*Garth*
- "Are you incompetent? Or do you just not care?" —*Debakey*

Other examples show us how drawing on grace helps us transform our thoughts and attitudes:

- "God blessed me with blindness. Now I see life in a way I could never see before." —*Vince*
- "I became angry with God and kept asking why. But God gave me more grace. He helped me see possibilities." —*Chrisford*
- "Well, I'm not special anymore, but I can be significant. I can make a difference." —*Elliot*
- "I want my daughters to know if they are susceptible to cancer. I don't want them to suffer like I have." —*Bernice*

Phrases	Common phrases	Thinking
Victim talk	If only	Others should fix things.
Zero talk	I can't or I haven't	I'm powerless to change things.
Hero talk	I can, I have, or I will	If I don't do it, it won't happen.
Grace talk	God can & I will cooperate	I do my part, God does His.

Words matter. Our verbal expressions give clues to the equation we use to process life. We can learn to evaluate our words and reflect on our thinking. We can ask, "what level of thinking do my words portray?"

If we tap into God's generosity, our thinking and words will change. And when our attitude changes, the way we respond to life's challenges will be transformed. In the following two chapters, we're going to explore our role in the equation.

- How do we draw on grace's work?
- What makes a third-level response unique?
- How do we express a faith response?

Questions to Assess your Level of Thinking
- *Who is in control?*
- *Who gets the credit?*
- *Who carries the burden?*
- *What is the source of my self-esteem?*
- *How am I esteeming myself in relation to God and others?*
- *What am I feeling?*
- *What do I fear?*
- *What language am I using?*

CHAPTER FIFTEEN

Taking Small Steps of Faith
Everyone believes something. On every level, a faith response exists. In a sense, response and faith are interchangeable.

    R represents responses.
    F represents faith.

$$R = F$$

Each level places confidence somewhere.

Level	Faith?	Faith's Focus	Help's source
Victim	Yes	Others	Outside Help
Hero/Zero	Yes	Self	Self Help
Grace	Yes	God	God Help

On the victim level, people place confidence in someone or something else. They expect a hero to intervene and save the day. Second-level thinkers believe in themselves. They trust in their skills, abilities, and know-how to navigate life. In their view, *self* has the power through

- self-determination,
- self-sufficiency,
- self-will, and
- self-actualization.

Since no one can escape believing, each thinker should ponder the source's credibility.

How reliable, effective, and trustworthy is the source where our confidence is placed?

First-level experiences remind us—people and programs let us down. The second level doesn't fare much better. We let ourselves down. The self doesn't have the capacity to overcome everything with self-responses.

On the third level, faith responses begin with God—not the self or other people. Grace thinkers place confidence in a God who is all-powerful, all-loving, and all-wise. They draw on God's help to do what they cannot.

And yet, grace responders understand they have a role to play. They must do their part. The focus shifts to cooperation: receiving and responding to God's generosity.

When I was a sophomore in college, three other students and I traveled to Mexico to visit a small medical clinic in the Yucatan. Knowing very little Spanish and nothing about medicine, we shadowed a wise doctor who cared for the Mayans living in the jungle. Dr. Perez taught us helpful lessons about medicine and patients.

One afternoon, wailing woke us from our siesta, Screams echoed through the clinic. We stumbled out of our hammocks and followed the sounds into the hallway. In the clinic foyer, nurses wrestled with a ten-year-old boy.

After a long battle, the nurses detached the bleeding boy from his mother and hauled him into the surgical area. We followed the nurses into the room, wondering what had happened to cause such chaos.

My three friends and I watched as four nurses tried to restrain the boy on a gurney. Strong and agile, the boy was winning the battle, breaking loose from their holds. While the boy yelled in Mayan, the head nurse, Arhelia, spoke to us in Spanish. "Es un laceration en la cabeza. Un machete."

Not understanding Arhelia, I walked closer. The screaming boy had a large gash on his forehead. Arhelia pointed at the bleeding wound. "Machete," she repeated.

Arhelia shooed the four of us into a corner and returned to restraining the Mayan boy. In defiance, he screamed at the top of his lungs. After a fight, the nurses strapped the boy down on the stretcher.

Dr. Perez entered the room, wiped the sleep from his eyes, and ran his hand through his hair. He walked over to the writhing boy. He calmly patted him on the shoulder and spoke to him in Mayan.

He snickered at the four of us trembling in the corner. "No préoccupe mis estudiantes. Es no problema."

I leaned toward my fellow students. "What did he say?"

"He said, 'Don't worry. It's no big deal,'" Alex whispered.

Dr. Perez washed his hands and put on his gloves while the boy squirmed, still trying to break free. "No mueve," commanded Perez, drawing anesthetic into a syringe. He then turned, smiled at me, and motioned. "Carlos, ayudame."

"What did he say?" I asked.

Before my friends could answer, Perez pointed to a pair of gloves and barked out another order. "Carlos, ayudame. Pon sus guantes."

I didn't know what he said, but I knew what he wanted. My name in Spanish was Carlos. I stood in the corner, afraid to move. Thoughts raced through my mind.

- I've never done this or seen anyone do this before.
- I'm unqualified. I've never been to medical school.
- I've never seen anyone suture anything.
- I've never practiced stitching.
- I'm not prepared. And he doesn't need my help.

My thoughts were interrupted by Perez asking, "Carlos. Que pasa? Ayudame."

Someone pushed me from behind. I stumbled forward, coaxed on by the doctor. After helping me put on sterile gloves, Perez took the anesthetic and injected it into the boy. The boy screeched and thrashed his head, pushing the needle deeper into his skin. Perez kept injecting, watching the boy's forehead swell.

Turning away from the boy, Perez began giving me pointers on how to suture. Drops of sweat formed on my face while he explained—in Spanish—how to place the needle through the skin.

Perez turned and pointed to our patient, who was now sleeping, exhausted from the fight. He smiled and motioned. "Carlos. Vamos."

The doctor placed the first stitch, explaining how to drive the needle through the skin. Then he tied down the knot. "Es fácil," he said, giving me the needle holder.

Dr. Perez took my hand and guided me through the first stitch. Then he showed me how the wrap the suture around the needle holder and pull down the knot. "No problema, Carlos."

After placing several stitches, he removed his hand and let me struggle. But with every stitch, I gained confidence. Before long, we closed the laceration.

Perez frowned. In a raspy voice, he mumbled, "Carlos. Sácalos."

Sácalos? I didn't know what he wanted.

Looking at the boy's head, it dawned on me. The sutures were not up to his standard. The botched repair looked like something from a Frankenstein movie.

Dr. Perez cut the sutures out. "Carlos. Sacalos suturas." He handed me the needle holder and pointed to the sleeping boy. "Otra vez."

With Dr. Perez's help, I closed the cut again. This time, the repair looked presentable.

"Muy bien, Carlos. Te gusta cirugía?" queried Perez.

Although I didn't recognize it at the time, this was a pivotal moment in my life. That experience caused something to click in my brain. I had taken my first step toward a destiny.

During medical school, I gravitated toward surgery and spent sleepless nights sewing up lacerations. I cared for trauma patients in the emergency room. I stayed to assist in surgery long after my shift had ended.

One experience led me down a path toward an outcome.

Reflecting on that moment, I wonder, *what if*? What if I had not responded and taken that first step? What if my mentor had closed the wound on his own without asking me to come along for the ride? This pivotal step launched me toward surgery. When I sutured the boy's laceration, I couldn't understand what was happening, but things began to make sense.

- I saw a tangible result or outcome.
- I enjoyed the risk, challenges—and chaos.
- I was challenged by learning repeatable skills.
- I liked being the hero and controlling situations.

An Invitation

Like Dr. Perez, who urged me to join him, grace coaxes us to take the first step. God doesn't need our help. He has all the resources and means to perform any task. Yet grace initiates the process, asking us to come, experience, and grow.

Invitations involve a relationship. Dr. Perez knew I didn't possess the skills or the confidence to fix the problem. Yet his support assured me that everything would turn out okay.

Jesus invited a group of rascals to come along and help him in his task. With each step, this odd bunch of victims, zeroes, and heroes soon learned to think differently about themselves, their circumstances, and their responses. The disciples learned dependence.

They learned to listen, cooperate, and obey—even when they didn't understand. Eventually, they became grace responders who made Jesus the hero of the story.

The invitation involves more than accomplishing a goal. Dr. Perez didn't step back, give me instructions, and expect me to perform the task independently, which would be a second-level approach. Dr. Perez came along with me and showed me the way.

Grace's appeal involves an assurance: a promise God will be with us, help us, and equip us as we step forward. Third-level responders focus on God's guarantee. With confidence, they step forward. They trust in a God who does what they cannot do for themselves. And then, by faith, they respond. The *G* factor is always working.

God initiates

- He has a plan, a blueprint. He possesses all the necessary resources to procure an outcome.

God invites

- He calls people to join his activity, to learn, and to grow.

God intervenes

- When our responses aren't enough, God steps in and helps.

God interrupts

- From our perspective, what looks like an about-face might be God's providence changing our direction to create a different outcome.

Lower-level Responses

Thinking on the lower levels, we often fail to step forward. Wearing victim lenses, we sometimes expect God to do *all* the work. We want God to intervene, while we don't need to lift a finger. Although God can—and sometimes does—deliver us from our circumstances, the third level involves a partnership.

In many cases, grace prods us forward so we can grow. Dr. Perez believed I could sew the boy's wound, and he wanted me to live up to my potential. Like Dr. Perez's invitation, Jesus's call brings us toward a meaningful outcome for both our benefit and God's glory.

Grace sees our potential—what we can become—and motions us to come and experience. At times, we approach God's bid to join him wearing our zero glasses. We believe we are inadequate. Thus, we make excuses and convince ourselves we aren't worthy.

I made many mental excuses for staying in the corner. Dr. Perez, aware of my incompetence, still asked for my help. In the same way, God understands our inadequacy. He doesn't expect us to perform anything in our own power. Grace is a gift in which we receive what is offered.

He wants us to draw on the *G* factor's help and experience his adequacy. We receive strength and understanding—whatever we need to fulfill the proposed outcome—as we move forward.

$C + R = O$ thinkers want to do something *for* God, focus on the task, and take the credit. We minimize the relationship and fixate on performance. God doesn't need our help. He wants to work *through* us to procure an outcome in which He receives the credit. A faith response requires a partnership.

- God invites us to join Him in His plans.
- We expect and draw on grace, trusting in God's help.
- God helps us and works through our circumstances.
- We enjoy freedom knowing God controls the outcome.
- We obey God's promptings and give him credit.

Every doctor in training goes through a process, a series of steps. The practice of medicine involves new challenges, experiences, and levels of growth. When doctors experience failure, they learn, get up, and try again. The goal isn't perfection, but direction.

My surgical journey began with a first step. Reluctantly, I moved forward, trusting Dr. Perez and responding to his invitation. I wasn't given a complete explanation or detailed description of how things would work out. The seasoned doctor asked me to come, see, and learn.

In the same way, God asks us to take the first step, one which requires a faith response. We trust God will keep his promise, be with us along the way, and help us moment by moment. This initial response involves understanding good and bad news. Before a physician discloses a treatment plan, he explains the diagnosis, thus beginning with the bad news first.

A Common Circumstance
Everyone shares a common situation. No matter how we picture ourselves, God sees us as zeroes. Our best responses will never measure up to his perfect standard. This disconnect fractures the relationship. This experience, common to all humankind, causes a spiritual separation.

C = *Separation and Spiritual Death*

Our feeble attempts to measure up to God's standards aren't enough to bring us back to God. Self-effort never procures the outcome God has for our lives. We are condemned for our poor responses and are held guilty because of our failures. God describes our inadequate responses with an intimidating word: sin.

This word evokes many negative emotions. The term comes from archery. When an arrow doesn't hit its mark, the archer has sinned. The aim has fallen short of the bullseye. This description explains how our best efforts fall short of God's expectations. Sin has an *i* in the middle for a reason. Sin involves

- placing ourselves in the center of the universe,
- saying we make the rules,
- thinking we are in control, and
- believing our goodness is good enough.

At its root, sin wants to be autonomous and trust in self. Our inadequate responses exclude the possibility of partnering with God. No matter how good they appear from our viewpoint, our efforts separate us from a third-level partnership. Because of our poor choices, we are separated from God.

Left to ourselves, we do not have the capacity to move toward God. We cannot experience the relationship for which we were designed, but instead of leaving us broken, God initiated the first step. Jesus helped us by taking our place and doing for us that which we couldn't do.

The G Factor Brings Good News

A cowboy took God up on his offer. When someone asked what had changed when he received God's help, the rancher explained things in a unique way.

"Well, it's pretty simple," said the man. "When I trusted Jesus, I felt like he stepped into my boots. And then I stepped into his. And now we share our boots."

In a funny way, the cowpoke explained a spiritual transaction. An exchange had occurred, one where Jesus had taken his place. When we receive God's generosity, Jesus steps into our life and places himself in our boots. He becomes our substitute, taking the punishment for our wrong actions and attitudes. Jesus takes our place and reconciles our relationship.

There's another part to the exchange. When we receive grace, we step into Jesus's boots. God changes his viewpoint, seeing us through the lenses of Jesus's perfection. We are infused with Jesus's life. We receive strength to respond and change our perception of circumstances.

Christ lives His life through us, instilling us with the *G* factor's power. This generous extension of grace comes through Jesus. This wonderful experience exchanges God's life for ours.

G = Jesus Takes Our Place and Extends Grace

Knowing our self-effort would never be enough, God gave us a way to reestablish our broken relationship. His response through Jesus is both adequate and just. Wrongs must be righted to restore fellowship. Our response to God's generosity begins by taking a step toward God. We receive a generous offer of restoration.

Two Possible Responses
We can respond to God's offer in one of two ways: we either accept or reject his help. We can trust that his solution is enough, or we can continue in self-effort, trust in our own performance, and live life on our own terms.

Here's a look at our possible responses in equation form:

R_1 = Trust in grace and take God's offer

R_2 = Trust in self and bear the responsibility

Not everyone chooses to take God's generosity, but many do. Some, the R_1 group, choose to step into Jesus's shoes, receive God's forgiveness, and cooperate, placing God into their equation. Those who don't, the R_2 group, decide to place themselves in the center, stay in control, and remain responsible for their performance.

Even Jesus's disciples chose different paths during his crucifixion. Peter made some poor choices. Wanting to be the hero, Peter made promises he couldn't keep. He vowed to be faithful to Jesus. Then Peter took events into his own hands by trying to fight Jesus's apprehenders.

Peter lied about knowing Jesus, something he had promised he would never do. Peter failed. His capital *R* quickly became a lowercase *r*. Peter felt ashamed. He felt like a zero.

The betrayal of Judas, another disciple, was more sinister. He snitched to the authorities and handed Jesus over to them. This act led to the death of an innocent man.

Both Peter and Judas, in their own ways, betrayed Jesus. Both had unacceptable performances. Zero responses. Each of the two disciples experienced guilt and shame. Both felt guilt over things they should and should not have done.

Judas chose the R_2 approach—a second-level response. He bore the burden of his poor responses alone. Feeling the weight of guilt and remorse, Judas chose a self-determined outcome. He chose suicide.

Peter embraced R_1—a third-level faith response. Although the fisherman failed, he took a different path. After Jesus rose from the dead, confirming his claim to be God, Peter took hold of grace. And grace took hold of Peter. Instead of carrying his burdens of guilt, Peter let Jesus bear them. Grace transformed Peter's outcome.

Jesus's invitation of grace had to be received. This step was a faith response—accepting Jesus's offer to bear his sin burden. Peter stepped forward, responding to Jesus's invitation to come along. He took the generous offer of forgiveness, acceptance, and restoration by faith. Peter received the gift offered by Jesus.

R_1 and R_2 lead to two distinct outcomes.

- R_1 leads to life.
- R_2 leads to death and spiritual separation from God.

Person	C	R	God's offer	Outcome
Peter	Betrayal	R_1	Accepted	God-determined
Judas	Betrayal	R_2	Rejected	Self-determined

TWO POSSIBLE RESPONSES

Stepping forward and taking God up on his invitation takes courage, but it's simple. Like the cowpoke explained, we trade boots. We give God our life, and he returns the favor. We receive what Christ has done for us and step in.

A third-level R1 approach requires bowing to a greater authority, giving up self-effort, changing our minds, and releasing control. For many second-level performers, taking this step is too costly. Second-level thinking tells us something doesn't add up. The offer is too good to be true.

Many don't step forward and receive grace for one reason. They reject God's terms because they feel they should do something to gain God's acceptance.

Instead of agreeing with God's assessment—that we can't and will never measure up—people choose their own way. They focus on a second-level response, trusting in their own performance. So, they choose R2—the safety of self-autonomy. In equation form, the two responses and their outcomes look like this:

Grace offered (C—separation + R1—accepting help) = Life
Grace offered (C—separation + R2—rejecting help) = Death

The first steps on any journey seem awkward. We feel overwhelmed and intimidated. Aware of our inadequacies, we fear stepping into the unknown.

When I lurched forward that day in Mexico, I had no idea what to expect and no clue where the path led. Although I didn't understand everything, I knew a skilled, kind doctor invited me to join him in his work.

Third-level thinkers see God's generosity call them forward: he initiates a work, interrupts the expected, intervenes in circumstances, and invites a response. Without understanding everything, they trust God to procure an outcome beyond imagination. By faith, they take grace's invitation and step into the moment.

A third-level response continues along the same vein. The second and third steps—and every footfall which follows—involve the same process. With an outcome in mind, God invites us in life's circumstances, and we respond.

The Christian life can't be lived on the second level. God doesn't call us and send us on a task alone, expecting us to rely on self-effort. Moment by moment, generosity comes along. God walks with us.

Faith is taking the first step even when you don't see the whole staircase.

Martin Luther King Jr.

CHAPTER SIXTEEN

Farmers, Bankers, and More Machetes

Seeds need more than water, sun, and soil. For seeds to produce, they must be cultivated. Growing a crop requires effort. Like seeds, grace must be cultivated.

Growing in grace, overcoming life obstacles, and responding in faith requires work. God does his part, and we must do ours. What is our part in the process?

The work required to cultivate a God-honoring outcome doesn't come through self-effort. Second-level responses fail to produce God's bounty. Grace thinkers harvest their crops through faith responses.

Sam and Ben, two neighboring farmers, planted crops. Both prayed God would bring rain. Sam sat on his porch, watched, and prayed. He didn't bother working his fields. Ben had a different approach. Ben got to work. He plowed the ground, pulled out the weeds, and planted fertilizer.

When the rain came, Ben's fields produced bountifully. Sam's didn't. At harvest time, Ben labored to bring in his crops. Sam, disappointed by the low yield, let crops waste away in the field.

What distinguished the two farmers? Ben and Sam had the same ground, sunshine, and rain. Both had the same number of hours to work their fields. Which one expressed the most faith?

Ben made the best of what he had received. He did his part and trusted God to do his. Half-hearted Sam had a lackadaisical attitude. He expected God to do all the work while he sat on the porch.

The same goes for doctors. Doctors can prescribe medicine, but they can't heal people. There are factors at work beyond a physician's control. Yet the doctor's role, practicing good medicine, is vital. The third level marries natural and supernatural elements. Our responses have significance. Our actions make a difference.

$G(C + R) = O$ operates in a unique way. Third-level performance doesn't flow from independence, self-effort, or striving. Slipping into these second-level responses places all the responsibility on self and fails to produce the outcome God desires.

Grace thinkers know that without the *G* factor, they cannot do things of spiritual significance. With humble confidence, they recognize their role in the process. Attitudes and actions do make a difference. On the third level, responses require cooperation by

- a partnership with God,
- an attitude of dependence, and
- an understanding of our inadequacy.

Cooperators take hold of the gifts, opportunities, and resources provided, and they draw upon grace. In return, God enlightens, equips, and empowers us to fulfill his purposes. And even when we fail, grace intervenes, moving events toward a God-defined outcome.

Grace is God's gift to us. How we return what is given reflects our grateful response back to God.

- How do we utilize grace?
- How do we optimize the *G* factor's potential—big or small—in our lives?

A faith response works with God and partners with Him in life events. Our degree of cooperation influences grace's potential to transform the outcome. On the third level, a faith response has several components.

What to Believe	How to respond
There are no coincidences. Happenings have purpose.	Accept reality
I am inadequate. God is adequate.	Acknowledge helplessness
God's way is better than my way	Adjust our thinking
God is already at work, setting things up	Anticipate God's activity

Acceptance

Faith faces reality. A faith response doesn't repress facts; it filters them through a framework of thought. Situations are viewed as they are, not the way we want them to be.

Faith moves beyond fatalism. Life events are not random cosmic accidents. They are placed in our lives with specificity and purpose by an all-loving God.

Joan, a forty-year-old bank executive, returned to the office for her biopsy results. I entered the exam room and watched her work. Like a circus juggler, she barked out orders over her cell phone, thumbed through loan documents, and wrote notes on a pad.

Oblivious to my presence, Joan continued. I sat down, reviewed the chart, and waited.

The banker looked up, startled. "Oh, I'm sorry. Things have been crazy at the bank."

Joan took control of the conversation. "What's the verdict?"

I spoke softly. "You have breast cancer."

The expression on her face flattened. Joan turned off her cell phone, closed her briefcase, and listened. While I explained treatment options, she returned a blank stare. I paused and gave her a tissue.

Instead of crying, she grimaced. "Doctor, I'm not going to receive that. Cancer is not God's will for my life."

Joan closed her briefcase, stood up, and walked out of the room. She never returned.

Cooperators may not welcome every life event. But heaven helps them accept reality. Beginning in this reality, grace thinkers look for God's activity. By faith, grace thinkers ask God to get them out or get them through, knowing that either outcome can fulfill God's purposes.

Either way, grace intervenes, provides the resources, and works through the circumstances. And faith takes hold of what is given, responds to challenges, and cooperates with the *G* factor.

Joan was trying to change reality. Instead of trusting God's providence, she had her own blueprint for things to turn out according to her expectations. Grace thinkers grasp what happens, find ways to tap into

God's favor, and trust in a meaningful outcome. When we move forward in this way, God takes responsibility for how things turn out.

Accepting life events doesn't mean we exclude God's intervention. Quite the opposite. Acceptance gives God room to respond in whatever way he chooses. Faith rests not in our desired result but in the one who holds the outcome.

Acknowledgment
Grace thinkers acknowledge their helplessness. Instead of working independently through self-effort, they recognize their limitations. When we fail to realize the inadequacy of our efforts and try to respond in our own strength, we often make things worse. Our faith shifts from God and moves self back into the center.

When I finished surgical training, I took the first position available. Determined to move ahead, I failed to see warning signs. I pushed forward, taking things into my own hands. I learned lessons the hard way. Things didn't fare well in my surgical practice. I encountered challenges for which I wasn't prepared.

I was swinging on the second-level see-saw, looking at events through hero lenses. When I hit bottom, realized my shortsightedness, and acknowledged my helplessness, I learned to draw on God's adequacy.

This zero experience helped me recognize my need to rely on God's strength instead of my own. My trust grew as I learned to agree with God, acknowledge my inadequacy, and ask for help.

Jesus responded to heroes and zeroes in different ways. Jesus confronted heroes who displayed self-confidence. He challenged religious individuals who seemed to have everything together.

Jesus expressed compassion for the weak responders. The lame, the deaf, the blind, and the outcasts—those who acknowledged their need—received his hand of grace.

What was a major difference between the two groups? Their level of acknowledgment.

The self-sufficient were unwilling to admit their helplessness. The zeroes, aware of their shortcomings and desperate for help, were willing to give up their self-reliance. Those who acknowledge their need are in a good place. From a third-level perspective, they are positioned to receive unmerited favor.

Grace thinkers adopt an *I can't, but God can through me* attitude.

Adjustment
The London Times once queried the greatest minds in England, asking them to expound on what was wrong in the world. Many noteworthy people sent in well-articulated responses.

Then the Times received a note from a journalist:

Dear Sirs: I am.

Sincerely Yours,

G. K. Chesterton

Chesterton's short, precise letter acknowledges we are often the source of our troubles. A faith adjustment begins with recognition that many of our troubles are self-induced. Shifting God into the center requires adjustments and faith.

Gabriel was a successful, middle-aged real estate executive. His income provided lots of things for his wife, Sally, and his son, Mateo. Gabe's life began to unravel. Mateo became an alcoholic. Sally had an affair with a co-worker. Gabe pointed fingers, but during counseling sessions he realized more fingers were pointing in his direction. The meetings exposed Gabriel's selfish attitudes.

Chasing material things created vacuums in Gabe's family. Sally needed Gabe's time, affection, and affirmation. Unable to receive Gabe's unconditional acceptance, Mateo tried to find his answers in a bottle.

Admitting his selfishness, Gabe asked God for help. And God gave him answers which required significant lifestyle changes. Gabe's adjustments paid big dividends as he walked through his circumstances. Gabe asked for forgiveness—from both God and his family. He cut back on work hours, spent time with his wife, and forgave her infidelity. He accompanied Mateo to Alcoholics Anonymous meetings.

When Gabe tapped into the *G* factor, his family's wounds began to heal. Gabe embraced the power of adjustment. "I've learned to love others—not fix them. God's love does the fixing. All I needed was to do was get in line with God."

Faith responders align their thinking with God's. Christians often use an intimidating word to describe this mental shift: repentance.

The essence of repentance means to change one's mind. We reject our assumptions and attitudes and adopt God's perspective. Lower-level thinkers often downplay the benefits of repentance. God's kindness urges us to adjust our attitude—not to hurt but to help us.

Third-level thinkers understand the rewards of changing their minds. Adjustments open the door for grace to change our circumstances. Gabe's adaptations brought emotional healing, restored relationships, spiritual growth, and a new beginning for his family.

Anticipation

Faith roots in hope, an expectation of the *G* factor's intervention. Grace thinkers are aware their circumstances don't surprise an all-knowing God. They know God's providence is already there, working to produce an outcome. Aware God doesn't intend to leave them in the dark, faith responders expect and search for God's activity. By faith, anticipators look for what God is already doing. They search for opportunities.

Anticipating God's move isn't passive. Anticipators listen, pray, seek wise counsel, study the Scriptures, and watch for open doors. When we look and listen, we often find grace already there, preparing the next step.

Acceptance, acknowledgment, adjustment, and anticipation aren't the only terms added to a third-level framework. A faith response requires cooperation.

Four Helpful Resources

Cooperators have multiple resources to draw upon to enhance their faith response. The Bible, the Holy Spirit, prayer, and other believers serve as channels through which grace thinkers draw strength.

Some have ill feelings toward the Bible. A book critic once wrote negative comments about a writer's work. In her opinion, everything about the book was wrong. One day, she met the author. They began to date. Their romance soon turned into marriage. The critic, after courtship, developed a new fondness for the author's book. What had changed? The critic got to know the author.

Our perspective about the Bible changes when we engage relationally with the author. It's more than historical evidence. The Scriptures guide our experiences, give us promises, remind readers of absolutes, and provide insight into our attitudes and actions. The Bible tells true stories of people's responses and the outcomes they encountered. The Scriptures are God's love letters written to us.

Help also comes from the Spirit of Christ, living within believers. This concept sounds strange to those unexposed to the Christian faith. It conjures ideas of aliens living inside, sucking the life out of people. The reverse is true. The indwelling Spirit gives life.

Christ's Spirit provides the means for God to work through them. The Spirit doesn't possess a third-level thinker and steal the freedom to choose. Individuals are still responsible for their own decisions. In a personal way, the Spirit guides individuals through life's choices, providing counsel and comfort.

The Spirit plants ideas and dreams into the minds of grace responders, bringing third-level creativity and resourcefulness. Christ's Spirit draws Scriptures and promises into our consciousness when the need arises. Working in tandem with the Bible, the Spirit prepares grace thinkers to participate in God's activity.

The third valuable resource is prayer. We ask for God's help, and he answers. The answer isn't always what we want, how we imagine it, or when we think it will happen. God promises to give us what we need for the outcome he intends.

The Bible gives examples of how to pray, when to pray, and what to pray for. And when we don't know what to pray or how to pray, the Spirit helps us.

We also need other believers. A community of third-level thinkers can encourage, pray, guide, and walk with us through our obstacles. We receive grace through others.

A faith response requires more than a single step of belief. One step leads to another and builds upon the last. Each stride advances us further, and each move is a response to God's invitation.

If we're teachable, we can learn with every step. My journey—both in the practice of surgery and in my faith walk—began as a college student. This process of growing in grace continues over a lifetime.

Another Machete at Bongolo

These days, I travel to Africa to fill in for doctors who train African surgeons. When I visit, I have opportunities to extend and receive grace.

- I face situations beyond my control where my faith responses are stretched.
- I learn to accept the circumstances, acknowledge my helplessness, adjust my life, and anticipate God's intervention.
- I learn to cooperate with God and with others.

Several years ago, I experienced another machete incident at Bongolo Hospital in Gabon. I had just arrived and was settling in to sleep when the phone rang.

Olivier, an intern who had just graduated from medical school, said, "Oui. Oui. Merci beaucoup, Dr. Chuck. We have a problem. Blood. Blood is everywhere."

"What happened?"

"An old lady fell on a machete," Olivier said. "Come quickly. I've called in the surgical team."

I put on my scrubs and walked down the hill in darkness, surrounded by jungle sounds. When I walked into the operating room, an older woman lay on the bed, unresponsive.

Olivier stood in a pool of blood, pressing on the lady's armpit with his hand. With his other, he held an oxygen mask over her face. "She fell on the machete several hours ago. She has almost bled to death."

"Where's the crew?" I asked.

"They are coming," replied Olivier. "And we have no blood."

"What?" I asked. "No blood at all?"

Olivier shook his head. "We don't see vascular injuries here at Bongolo. They usually die before they arrive at the hospital."

When I gently pulled Olivier's hand away, blood spurted out of the woman's armpit.

"Where's the scrub nurse?" I took over and applied pressure on the wound.

"We have no help tonight. It's just us." Olivier pulled supplies off shelves and set up the surgical table while I held pressure.

"We'll need vascular clamps and some 4/0 sutures."

Olivier left the room to search for supplies. The anesthetist entered, looked at the unconscious patient, turned around, and walked out of the room.

"This is not going to go well," I mumbled.

Olivier returned with large clamps and sutures. The suture needles were too large to be used on the small vessels.

"Olivier, these won't work. We need a smaller needle," I said.

"I'll keep looking."

"And Olivier, these are aortic clamps. They're too big. The axillary artery is the size of my pinky finger."

Olivier nodded and hustled away. I sighed, relieved, when the anesthetist returned with his tools. "I'm so glad you're back. I thought you had run off to hide."

The anesthetist said nothing and put the woman to sleep. Soon, Olivier returned, bringing sutures with smaller needles.

Seeing a glimmer of hope, I commanded Olivier to go outside and wash his hands. At the same time, I held pressure and prepped the woman for surgery.

When Olivier returned, I said, "Olivier, now it's your turn. Hold pressure and drape the patient while I go outside and scrub."

The intern interrupted my command. "Oui, Dr. Chuck. We must pray first."

My head began to spin. This was the time to act—not pray. Before I could speak, Olivier bowed his head. "Lord, thank you for this opportunity. Nothing catches you by surprise. Help us to help this lady. We love you, Oh Lord, our strength."

Glad Olivier kept it short and sweet, I ran outside and washed my hands, reflecting on his prayer.

While scrubbing, I thought about the last words of his prayer. *We love you, Oh Lord, our strength.* I realized those words came from a Psalm in the Bible. David, the boy who took down Goliath with stones and a sling, wrote those words. How did David do it?

David's strength came from a source greater than himself. David tapped into grace, trusting God to intervene in the battle. Yet David had to use the tools provided in the moment.

Returning to the room, I realized my mind was fixated on all the wrong things—the items I didn't have. Too few resources. No blood. The lack of experienced help. Clamps and needles in the wrong sizes. An older woman lacking the reserve to tolerate the surgery. A situation I believed was a set-up for failure.

I had failed to see the greatest resource in the room. Grace. I realized that with God's help, I had everything I needed. David didn't focus on his lack of resources. Small stones and a slingshot were enough, with a God-centered equation.

I needed to shift my thinking, do my best, and draw on the source of help. God had already provided what I needed to produce the outcome. I was bearing stressful burdens God didn't intend for me to carry. Olivier's prayer extended grace to me and helped me focus on the tools I already had. Christ's Spirit reminded me of David, drawing my focus back to the greatest resource in the universe.

That night, things didn't add up. Two plus two equaled much more than expected. Another factor was working, which I cannot take the credit for: grace. God would do his part, but I needed to cooperate. When I cooperated and made mental adjustments, I gave grace permission to work in the situation.

Somehow, Olivier and I repaired the woman's artery and vein with few earthly resources. That evening, I learned a lesson: grace is enough. What I needed more than resources was a change of mind: the ability to see the event through $G(C + R) = O$ lenses.

Often, we don't realize God is all we need until God is all we have. Everything to procure the outcome had been provided. Like David, I had to take what I had been given. I didn't need first-world resources any more than David needed an army to defeat a giant. All we needed was God's help.

God expressed grace, starting with Olivier's prayer, to give me all the tools needed for the challenge. That evening, I had to utilize all the elements of a faith response. And God's generosity showed up with help.

- I had to *accept* the circumstances beyond my control and release the outcome.
- Olivier's prayer caused me to *acknowledge* my inadequacy and desperation.
- The Bible verse helped me *adjust* my attitude and thoughts about the event.
- I learned to *anticipate* God's provision in the crisis with the Spirit's leading.
- I learned to *cooperate* with God and Olivier, working toward a purposeful end.

The *G* factor brings new dimensions into our thinking. Second level resources—creativity, ingenuity, adaptability—flow from a source greater than ourselves. The life equation rises out the lower ones and changes our thinking. This experience continues as grace and faith work together for a God-honoring outcome.

Sow a thought and you reap an action; sow an act and you reap a habit; sow a habit and you reap a character; sow a character and you reap a destiny.

Ralph Waldo Emerson

YOUR FORMULA AND YOUR STORY

Most historians say Einstein was terrible at math. When the physicist presented his cosmological constant, he divided it by zero—a blunder most sixth graders can recognize. Although he may have made some mathematical errors, he proved his brilliance with thought experiments. Using this technique, the physicist could translate abstract ideas into formulas.

Einstein created mental pictures of his theories and then jumped into them. This method helped him explain abstract concepts in ways others could understand. Need I mention $E = mc2$?

Einstein placed himself in his equations. Pretending to be a particle moving at the speed of light, the physicist whisked around the room and imagined how the formula would affect things. Using these visual techniques, he asked questions, made observations, and developed theories about the universe. Living in his equations, Einstein understood space, time, and energy.

Everyone has a story, and everyone has a formula. I'm a surgeon with crazy life experiences and equations running through my brain. I've shared personal snippets from my life and things I've learned from others, and I've shared a bunch of formulas. By now, you know—like Einstein, I have some mathematical challenges.

I have attempted to help get these formulas into your head one spoonful at a time by using stories. Or perhaps, like Einstein, I have tried to get *you* into the formulas. These equations provide a visual grid to help you frame your story.

What's Your Formula?

These equations don't present an airtight understanding of worldviews. These expressions help us understand the big picture. No one is forcing you to believe in $G(C + R) = O$. These formulas merely help you understand *why* this third level of thinking is needed and *how* one lives in it. It marries reason and faith, evidence and experience, the natural and the supernatural, God's part and our part.

The Christian experience isn't formulaic. It's relational, defined by grace.

- Some think the life equation is a means to getting the outcome they desire, but they're not getting the big picture.
- Some want a formula to replace a personal relationship with God, the author of grace, but they've missed the point.
- Some desire to plug in a programmed response to conjure health, happiness, and wealth. They approach the formula with second-level lenses.
- Some think the story still revolves around themselves, but they don't understand the principles.

What's Your Story?
Hopefully, these stories have helped you connect with yourself—and God—in a new way. As you reflect on your life story, I'd like to remind you of these truths:

- you don't have to be a victim,
- you don't have to be a zero, and
- you don't have to be a hero.

You have another option. You can embrace the third level of thinking. You can receive God's offer of grace. Once we step into *The Life Equation* and live in it, our experiences change.

The Christian life has been expressed in many ways and may confound the most brilliant minds. The basics are simple. $G(C + R) = O$ helps us wrap our minds around what God has done, is doing, and will do.

The *G* factor introduces God's response into our mental framework. Once we understand that God is willing and able to do what we cannot do for ourselves, our thinking changes. Grace invites us to step into the equation. A third-level response can be simplified. God gives. And by faith, we utilize what we have received.

WHAT'S YOUR STORY?

Grace (Faith) = Outcome

God offers unmerited favor. We must receive, apply, and practice it. We are given the opportunity to respond by taking what grace provides. When we enter this exciting dimension, our focus shifts. We no longer play the leading role in our life's drama. Our story, with its twists, trials, and triumphs, becomes part of a greater narrative.

Third-level thinkers believe their adventures contribute to God's grander story. All of history is *his* story. God's the hero in the drama. The story expresses grace: God's response for us. Now that's a story to tell.

When facing a life challenge, let's stop a moment to ponder.

- What level of thinking do I use to process my life events?
- Am I wearing grace lenses, or am I thinking like a victim?
- Am I allowing grace to influence the way I process my circumstances?
- Do I see myself as a victim, a zero, a hero, or a grace thinker?

When we consider our responses, let's ask ourselves a few questions.

- What source do I employ for help—myself or God?
- Do I acknowledge my responses as adequate or inadequate?
- What adjustments do I need to make to draw upon God's help?
- How do I see hints of God's activity in my life events?
- Am I cooperating with God and utilizing a faith response?

When we imagine the outcome, let's consider our formulas.

- What elements do I place in my formula to evaluate the outcome?
- Am I making room for God to define the outcome?
- Do I want to control the outcome or am I willing to release it?

Emerson's second-level quote has third-level implications. Our thoughts—the formulas in our minds—impact our ultimate outcome. Clear thinking creates a cascade of habits and character. And ultimately, these thoughts ripple into our destiny. Which factors and terms will define your formula and your story?

We can choose our formula and our story. I have chosen a life defined by grace. I have chosen the life equation and placed my story into God's grander narrative. Which will you embrace?

> He who did not spare his own Son, but gave him up for us all—how will he not also, along with him, graciously give us all things?

Paul the Apostle
Romans 8:32

BIBLIOGRAPHY

Alcorn, R. (2014). *If God Is Good: Faith in the Midst of Suffering and Evil.* Multnomah Books.

Behe, M. J. (1996). *Darwin's Black Box: The Biochemical Challenge to Evolution.* Free Press. Free Press Free Press.

Behe, M. J. (2019). *Darwin Devolves: The New Science About DNA That Challenges Evolution.* HarperOne, An Imprint of HarperCollins Publishers.

Canfield, J., & Switzer, J. (2017). *The Success Principles: How to Get from Where You Are to Where You Want to Be.* Thorsons.

Colson, C. W., & Pearcey, N. (1999). *How Now Shall We Live?: Study Guide.* Tyndale House Publishers.

Geisler, N. L., & Hoffman, P. K. (2006). *Why I Am a Christian: Leading Thinkers Explain Why They Believe.* Baker Books.

Geisler, N. L., & Turek, F. (2007). *I Don't Have Enough Faith to Be an Atheist.* Crossway Books.

Henry Wadsworth Longfellow. (n.d.). *A Psalm of Life.* Ernest Nister; New York.

Jastrow, R. (1992). *God and the Astronomers.* Norton.

Keller, T. (2016). *The Reason for God: Belief in an Age of Skepticism.* Penguin.

Lewis, C. S. (2017). *Mere Christianity.* HarperCollins Publishers.

Little, P. E. (2008). *Know Why You Believe.* Intervarsity Press.

McDowell, J. (1981). *More evidence that demands a verdict: Historical Evidences for the Christian Scriptures.* Here's Life Publishers.

McDowell, J. (1999). *Evidence That Demands a Verdict.* Thomas Nelson Publishers.

Meyer, S. C. (2020). *The Return of the God Hypothesis: Compelling Scientific Evidence for the Existence of God.* New York, Ny: HarperOne.

Meyer, U., & Coffey, W. R. (2015). *Above the Line: Lessons in Leadership and Life from a Championship*. Penguin Audio.

Michael Rosen performs *We're Going on a Bear Hunt*. (2014). [YouTube Video]. In *YouTube*. https://www.youtube.com/watch?v=0gyI6ykDwds

Paley, W. (2015). *Natural Theology: or, Evidences of the Existence and Attributes of the Deity, Collected from the Appearances of Nature*.

Pan-African Academy of Christian Surgeons: Home. (n.d.). Paacs.net. Retrieved March 26, 2022, from https://paacs.net/

Poetry Foundation. (2018). *Poetry Foundation*. Poetry Foundation. https://www.poetryfoundation.org/poems/51642/invictus

Schaeffer F. (1990). *Francis Schaeffer Trilogy*. Inter-Varsity Press.

Strobel, L. (2004). *The Case for a Creator: A Journalist Investigates Scientific Evidence That Points Toward God*. Zondervan.

Tournier, P. (1984). *The Strong and the Weak*. Highland.

About the Author

It would be simple to portray Dr. Charles Page, MD, as just a country surgeon. But that would be missing way too much. Dr. Chuck (that's what everyone calls him) has developed a methodology for everyday people to navigate life's inevitable tragedies and triumphs and to have a deeper understanding of why they respond to these events the way they do.

Through his book, videos, and TV shows, Dr. Chuck peers into the everyday lives of people struggling and thriving in rural East Texas. He comes along at a time when Americans—and the world for that matter—are going through confusing changes, such as aging demographics and new technology which changes how we work and live.

With scarce resources in rural medicine, Dr. Chuck faces complications and puts in the extra work to ensure his patients receive the best medical care. Sometimes he works seven days a week, checking on patients in the early morning or late evening hours while fighting the corporate stranglehold on healthcare. Still, Dr. Chuck says he wouldn't give up his freedom to work for himself and will not be beholden to a system which often doesn't put the patient first.

Dr. Chuck has created a view of life which reflects the challenges and setbacks of the patients who have entered his office. Many lack wealth and the basic resources needed to lead their fullest lives. Dr. Chuck has developed equations, or formulas, to help explain the human condition with the hope of awakening positive outcomes in people's lives.

Dr. Chuck comes from a Christian evangelical background. Still, his message rings true for those not connected to a specific religious denomination or even for those with a secular mindset. He lives in and embraces the diversity of his hometown of Nacogdoches in East Texas. He holds prayer meetings and biblical discussion for college students from the

United States, Mexico, Central America, and Africa. He works to help the students find direction and happiness in their lives in an increasingly complex and challenging world.

Dr. Chuck is a proud graduate of the prestigious Baylor College of Medicine, where he also completed his internship and residency. He was fortunate to be able to train under pioneering surgeon Dr. Michael Ellis Debakey, whose discoveries influenced medicine in the twentieth century.

When he's not in doctor and mentor mode, Chuck loves spending time with his wife, Joanna, and their children—Jacob, Jonathan, Georgia, Jane Aubrey, and Charlie.

To connect with Dr. Chuck and to receive updates:
text "spoonful" to 66866.

For an overview of the principles in this book, click below and register. When you sign up, you'll receive

- four short videos which explain the ways we see our circumstances and the ways in which we respond,
- a framework to transform your challenges into blessings and
- updates from the Spoonful of Courage TV show.

Register here for FOUR free videos